RUDOLF STEINER (1861–1925) called his spiritual philosophy 'anthroposophy', meaning 'wisdom of the human being'. As a highly developed seer, he based his work on direct knowledge and perception of spiritual dimensions. He initiated a modern and universal 'science of spirit', accessible to anyone willing to exercise clear and unprejudiced thinking.

From his spiritual investigations Steiner provided suggestions for the renewal of many activities, including education (both general and special), agriculture, medicine, economics, architecture, science, philosophy, religion and the arts. Today there are thousands of schools, clinics, farms and other organizations involved in practical work based on his principles. His many published works feature his research into the spiritual nature of the human being, the evolution of the world and humanity, and methods of personal development. Steiner wrote some 30 books and delivered over 6,000 lectures across Europe. In 1924 he founded the General Anthroposophical Society, which today has branches throughout the world.

THE FOUR SEASONS AND THE ARCHANGELS

Experience of the Course of the Year in Four Cosmic Imaginations

Five lectures given in Dornach, Switzerland, between 5 and 13 October 1923

RUDOLF STEINER

Translation revised by Pauline Wehrle

RUDOLF STEINER PRESS

Rudolf Steiner Press
Hillside House, The Square
Forest Row, East Sussex
RH18 5ES

www.rudolfsteinerpress.com

First edition 1947
Second edition 1968
Third edition 1984; reprinted 1992
Fourth edition 1996; reprinted 2002, 2008

Originally published in German (with six lectures) under the title *Das Miterleben des Jahreslaufes in vier kosmischen Imaginationen* (volume 229 in the *Rudolf Steiner Gesamtausgabe* or Collected Works) by Rudolf Steiner Verlag, Dornach. This authorized translation published by kind permission of the Rudolf Steiner Nachlassverwaltung, Dornach

Translation © Rudolf Steiner Press 1996

A catalogue record for this book is available from the British Library

ISBN 978 185584 050 8

Cover by Andrew Morgan incorporating Russian orthodox icon, 'Synaxis of Archangel Michael'
Typeset by DP Photosetting, Aylesbury, Bucks.
Printed and bound in Great Britain by 4edge Limited, Essex

Contents

Foreword

In these lectures, given to an audience largely familiar with Anthroposophy,* Rudolf Steiner speaks particularly to our hearts and to our active desire to participate in the life of nature. We are led out of our narrow selves further than we may ever have dreamed of, until we not only feel and share the rising life of spring but also make the acquaintance of the forces and beings active there. Yet we can feel these imaginations to be real in a deeper way than life on the surface, and we encounter as we go along many an insight into secrets of physics and chemistry and revelations about the origins and meaning of art. Indeed, we meet in these lectures many striking thoughts, one or another of which may well trigger a memory deep inside us.

If we are prepared to go along with the experiences described here, the changing seasons will never be a 'dull round' again, and we shall become more aware of the subtle differences in ourselves as we come closer to living nature in the spring and summer, and become more truly our-selves—within our own individual personalities—in the autumn and winter.

Pauline Wehrle

*See Publisher's Note on page 73.

Lecture 1

THE MICHAEL IMAGINATION

Today I would like first to remind you how events that take place behind the veil of appearance, outside the physical, sense-perceptible world, can be described in pictorial terms. One has to speak in this way of these events, but the pictures correspond throughout with reality.

With regard to sense-perceptible events, we are living in a time of hard tests for humanity—and these tests will become harder still. Many old forms of civilization, to which people still mistakenly cling, will sink into the abyss, and there will be an insistent demand that mankind must find its way to something new. In speaking of the course that the external life of humanity will take in the near future we cannot—as I have often said—arouse any kind of optimistic hopes. But a valid judgment as to the significance of external events cannot be formed unless we also consider the determining, directing cosmic events that occur behind the veil of the senses.

When we look out attentively with our physical eyes and our other senses at our surroundings we perceive the physical environment of the earth and the various kingdoms of nature within it. This is the milieu in which comes to pass all that manifests as wind and weather in the course of the year. When we direct our senses towards the external world we have all this before us. These are the external facts. But behind the atmosphere, the sun-illumined atmosphere, there lies another world, perceptible by spiritual organs, as we may call them. Compared with the sense world this other world is a higher world, a world wherein a kind of light, a kind of spiritual light or astral light, spiritual existence and spiritual deeds shine out and run their course. And they are in truth no less significant for the whole development of the world and of mankind than the historical events in the external environment of the earth and on its surface.

If anyone today is able to penetrate into these astral realms, wandering through them as one may wander among woods and mountains and find signposts at cross-roads, he may find 'signposts' there in the astral light, inscribed in spiritual script. But these signposts have a quite special characteristic: they are not comprehensible without further explanation, even for someone who can 'read' in the astral light. In the spiritual world and in its communications things are not made as convenient as possible: anything one encounters there presents itself as a riddle to be solved. Only through inner investigation, through experiencing inwardly the riddle and much else, can one discover what the inscription on a spiritual signpost signifies.

And so at this time — indeed for some decades now, but particularly at this time of hard trials for mankind — one can read in the astral light, as one goes about spiritually in these realms, a remarkable inscription. It sounds like a prosaic comparison, but in this case, because of its inner significance, it does not remain prosaic. Just as we find notices to help us find our way — and we find signposts even in poetic landscapes — we encounter an important spiritual signpost in the astral light. Time and time again, exactly repeated, we find there today the following message inscribed in highly significant spiritual script:

O Man,
You shape it to your service,
You display it according to the value of its substance
In many of your products.
Yet it will only make you whole
When it reveals to you
The exalted dominion of its spirit.

Injunctions of this kind, pointing to facts significant for mankind, are inscribed, as I have said, in the astral light, presenting themselves first as a kind of riddle to be solved, so that human beings may bring their soul forces into activity.

Now, let us contribute something to the solving of this inscription — really a simple inscription, but important for mankind today.

Let us recall how in many of our studies here we have surveyed the course of the year. One first observes it quite externally: when spring comes one sees nature sprouting and budding; one watches the plants grow and come to flower and sees how life everywhere springs up out of the soil. All this is enhanced as summer draws on; in summer it rises to its highest level. And then, when autumn comes, it withers and fades away; and when winter comes it dies into the bosom of the earth.

This cycle of the year — which in earlier times, when a more instinctive consciousness prevailed, was celebrated with festivals — has another aspect, also mentioned here. During winter the earth is united with the elemental spirits. They withdraw into the interior of the earth and live there among the plant roots preparing for new growth, and among the other nature beings who spend the winter there. Then, when spring comes, the earth breathes out, as it were, its elemental being. The elemental spirits rise up as though from a tomb and ascend into the atmosphere. During winter they conformed to the inner order of the earth, but now, as spring advances and especially when summer comes on, they open themselves to the order that is imposed upon them by the stars and the movements of the stars. When midsummer has come then out there in the periphery of the earth life surges among the elemental beings who had spent the winter quietly and calmly under the earth's mantle of snow. In the swirling and whirling of their dance they are governed by the reciprocal laws of planetary movement, by the pattern of the fixed stars, and so on. When autumn comes, they turn towards the earth. As they approach the earth they become subject more and more to the laws of the earth, so that in winter they may be breathed in again by the earth, once more to rest there in tranquillity.

Anyone who can thus experience the cycle of the year feels that his whole human life is wonderfully enriched. Today — and for some time past — a person normally experiences, though but dimly, half-consciously, only the physical-etheric processes of the body taking place within his skin. He experiences his breathing, the circulation of his blood. Everything that takes its course outside, in wind and weather during the year, all that lives in the sprouting of the seed forces, the fruiting of the earth forces, the brilliance of the sun forces — all this is no less significant and decisive for the whole life of a human being, even though he is not conscious of it, than the breathing and blood circulation which goes on inside his skin.

As the sun rises over any region of the earth we share in what it brings out by means of its warmth and light. And when a person accepts anthroposophy in the right sense, not reading it like a sensational novel but so that what it imparts fills his mind and heart, then he gradually educates himself, heart and soul, to experience all that goes on outside in the course of the year. Just as during a day we experience early freshness, readiness to work in the morning, then the onset of hunger, and weariness in the evening, and just as we can sense the inner life and activity of the forces and substances within our skin so, by taking to heart anthroposophical ideas — entirely different from the usual descriptions of sense-perceptible events — we can prepare our souls to become open to the activities that go on outside in the course of the year. We can deepen more and more this empathy with sympathetic participation in the cycle of the year, and we can enrich it so that we do not live so cut off within our skin, letting the outer world pass us by. But on the contrary, we can enrich our experience so that we feel ourselves living in the blossoming of every flower, in the breaking open of the buds, in that wonderful secret of the morning, in the glistening of dewdrops in the rays of the sun. In these ways we can get beyond that dull, conventional way of reacting to the outer world merely by putting on our overcoat in winter and lighter clothes in summer and taking an umbrella when it rains. When we overcome a prosaic attitude and learn to experience the interweaving activities, the ebb and flow, of nature — only then do we really understand the cycle of the year.

Then, when spring passes over the earth and summer is drawing near, we will be heart and soul in the midst of it; we will perceive how the sprouting and budding life of nature unfolds, how the elemental spirits whirr and whirl in a pattern laid down for them by planetary movements. And then, in the time of high summer, we too will widen our experience to share in the life of the cosmos. Certainly this damps down our own inner life, but at the same time our summer experiences lead us out — in a cosmic waking sleep, one might say — to enter into the activities of the planets.

Today, generally speaking, people feel they can enter into the life of nature only in the season of growth — of germination and budding, flowering and fruiting. Even if they cannot fully experience all this, they have more sympathetic awareness of it than of the autumn season of fading and withering. But in truth we deserve to rejoice in the season of spring growth only if we can enter also into the time when summer wanes and autumn approaches, the season of sinking down and dying that comes with winter. And if at midsummer we rise inwardly, in a cosmic waking sleep, with the elemental beings to the regions where planetary activity in the outer world can be inwardly experienced, then we ought also to sink ourselves down under the frost and snow mantle of winter, so that we enter into the secrets of the womb of the earth during midwinter; and we ought to participate in the fading and dying off of nature when autumn begins.

If, however, we are to participate in this waning of nature, just as we do in nature's growing time, we must learn to experience the dying away of nature in our own inner being. For if a person becomes more sensitive to the secret workings of nature, and thus participates actively in nature's germinating and fruiting, it follows that he will also livingly experience the effects of autumn in the outer world. But it would be comfortless for a human being if he could experience this only in the form it takes in nature; if he were to come only to a nature-consciousness concerning the secrets of autumn and winter as he readily does concerning the secrets of spring and summer. When the events of autumn and winter draw on, when Michaelmas comes, he certainly must enter sensitively into the processes of fading and dying. But he must not, as he does in summer, give himself over to nature-consciousness. On the contrary, he must then devote himself to self-consciousness. In the time when external nature is dying, he must oppose nature-consciousness with the force of self-consciousness.

And then the form of Michael stands before us again. If, under the impulse of anthroposophy, a person enters thus into the enjoyment of nature, the consciousness of nature, but then also awakes in himself an autumnal self-consciousness, the picture of Michael with the dragon will stand majestically before him, revealing in picture form the overcoming of nature-consciousness by self-consciousness when autumn draws near. This will come about if humanity can experience not only an inner spring and summer but also a dying, death-bringing inner autumn and winter. Then it will be possible for the picture of Michael with the dragon to appear again as a powerful Imagination, summoning humanity to inner activity.

For a person who through present-day spiritual knowledge wrestles his way through to an experience of this picture it expresses something very powerful. For when, after St John's-tide, July, August and September draw on, he will come to realize how he has been living through a waking sleep of inner planetary experience in company with the earth's elemental beings, and he will become aware of what this really signifies.

It signifies an inner process of combustion, but we must not picture it as being like external combustion. All the processes that take a definite form in the outer world take place also within the human organism, but in a different way. And so it is a fact that the changing course of the year is reflected in these inner processes.

The inner process that occurs during high summer is a permeation of the organism by what crudely may be described in the material world as sulphur. When a person lives with the summer sun and its effects, he experiences a sulphurizing process in his physical-etheric being. The sulphur that he bears within him as a useful substance has a special importance for him in high summer, quite different from its importance at other seasons. It becomes a kind of combustion process. It is natural for mankind that the sulphur process in us at midsummer should be specially enhanced. Material substances in different beings have secrets not dreamt of by materialistic science.

Everything physical-etheric in us is thus glowed through at midsummer with inward sulphur fire, to use Jakob Boehme's expression. It is a gentle, intimate process, imperceptible to ordinary consciousness, but—as is generally true of other such processes—it has a tremendous, decisive significance for events in the cosmos.

Although this sulphurizing process in human bodies at midsummer is so mild and gentle and imperceptible to mankind itself, it has a very great importance for the evolution of the cosmos. A great deal happens out there in the cosmos when in summer human beings shine inwardly with the sulphur process. It is not only the physically visible glow-worms (*Johanniskaeferchen*) which shine out around St John's Day. For other planets the inner being of mankind then begins to shine, becoming visible as a being of light to the etheric eyes of other planetary beings. That is the sulphurizing process. At the height of summer human beings begin to ray out into cosmic space as brightly for other planetary beings as glow-worms shine with their light in the meadows at St John's time.

From the standpoint of the cosmos this is a majestically beautiful sight, for it is in glorious astral light that human beings shine out into the cosmos during high summer, but at the same time it gives occasion for the ahrimanic power to draw near to mankind. For this power is very closely related to the sulphurizing process in the human organism. We can see how, on the one hand, human beings shine out into the cosmos in the St John's light, and on the other how the dragonlike serpent form of Ahriman winds its way among the human beings shining in the astral light and tries to ensnare and embrace them, to draw them down into the realm of subconscious sleep and dreams. Then, caught in this web of illusion, they would become world dreamers, and in this condition they would be a prey to the ahrimanic powers. All this has significance for the cosmos also.

And when in high summer from a particular constellation meteors fall in great showers of cosmic iron, then this cosmic iron, which carries an especially powerful healing force, is the weapon which the gods bring to bear against Ahriman as, dragonlike, he tries to coil round the shining forms of human beings. The force which falls on the earth in meteoric iron is indeed a cosmic force whereby the higher gods endeavour to gain a victory over the ahrimanic powers, when autumn comes on. And this majestic display in cosmic space, when the August meteor showers stream down into human beings shining in the astral light, has its counterpart—so gentle and apparently so small—in a change that occurs in the human blood. This human blood, which is in truth not so material as present-day science imagines but is permeated throughout by impulses of soul and spirit, is rayed through by the force that is carried as iron into the blood and wages war there on anxiety, fear and hate. The processes set going in every blood corpuscle when the force of iron shoots into it are the same, on a minute human scale, as those which take place when meteors fall in a shining stream through the air. This permeation of human blood by the anxiety-dispelling force of iron drives fear and anxiety out of the blood.

And so as the gods with their meteors wage war on the spirit who would like to spread fear over all the earth by way of his coiling serpent form, and they cause iron to irradiate this fear-tainted atmosphere which is at its peak when autumn approaches or when summer wanes — so the same process occurs inwardly in human beings when their blood is permeated with iron. We can understand these things only if on the one hand we understand their inner spiritual significance and, on the other, we recognize how the sulphur process and the iron process in mankind are connected with corresponding events in the cosmos.

A person who looks out into space and sees a shooting star should say to himself, with reverence for the gods: 'What is happening in the great expanse of space has its minute counterpart continuously in myself. Out there are the shooting stars, while in every one of my blood corpuscles iron is taking form; my life is full of shooting stars, miniature shooting stars.' And this inner fall of shooting stars, which in truth signifies the life of the blood, is especially important when autumn approaches, when the sulphur process is at its peak. For when human beings are shining like glow-worms in the way I have described, then the counter-force is present also, for millions of tiny meteors are scintillating inwardly in their blood.

This is the connection between the inner man and the universe. And then we can see how, especially when autumn is approaching, there is a great raying upwards of sulphur from the nerve system towards the brain. One could say that the whole human being can then be seen as a sulphur-illuminated phantom.

But raying into this bluish-yellow sulphur atmosphere come the meteor swarms from the blood. That is the other phantom. While the sulphur phantom rises in clouds from the lower part of the human being towards the head, the iron-forming process rays out from his head and pours like a stream of meteors into the life of the blood.

Such is the human being when Michaelmas draws near. And we must learn to make conscious use of the meteoric force in our blood. We must learn to keep the Michael festival by making it a festival of fearlessness, a festival of inner strength and initiative—a festival for the commemoration of selfless self-consciousness.

Just as at Christmas we celebrate the birth of the Redeemer and at Easter the death and resurrection of the Redeemer, and as at St John's-tide we celebrate the outpouring of human souls into cosmic space, so at Michaelmas—if the Michael festival is to be rightly understood— we must celebrate what lives spiritually in the sulphurizing and meteorizing process within us and should appear to human consciousness in its whole soul-spiritual significance especially at Michaelmas. Then a person can say to himself: 'You will be master of this process, which otherwise takes its natural course outside your consciousness, if—just as you bow down thankfully before the birth of the Redeemer at Christmas and experience Easter with deep inner response—you learn to experience how at this autumn festival of Michael there should grow in you everything that opposes love of ease, opposes anxiety, and encourages the unfolding of inner initiative and free, strong, courageous will.' The festival of strong will—that is how we should conceive of the Michael festival. If that is done, then if nature knowledge is true, spiritual, human self-consciousness, the Michael festival will shine out in its true colours.

But before mankind can think of celebrating the Michael festival there will have to be a renewal in human souls. It is the renewal of our whole soul disposition that should be celebrated at the Michaelmas festival — not as an outward or conventional ceremony, but as a festival that renews the whole inner man.

Then, out of all I have described, the majestic image of Michael and the dragon will arise once more. It will paint itself out of the cosmos. The dragon paints itself for us, forming its body out of bluish-yellow sulphur streams. We see it taking shape in shimmering clouds of radiance out of the sulphur vapours; and over the dragon rises the figure of Michael, Michael with his sword.

But we shall picture this rightly only if we see the space where Michael displays his power and his lordship over the dragon as filled not with indifferent clouds but with showers of meteoric iron. These showers take form from the power that streams out from Michael's heart; they fuse into the sword of Michael who overcomes the dragon with his sword of meteoric iron.

If we understand what is happening in the universe and in mankind, then the cosmos itself will paint from out of its own forces. Then the artist does not lay on this or that colour arbitrarily but, in harmony with divine powers and with the world that expresses their being, he paints the whole being of Michael and the dragon, as it can hover before one. A renewal of the old pictures comes about if one can paint out of direct contemplation of the cosmos. Then the pictures will show what is really there, and not what fanciful individuals may somehow imagine to be a picture of Michael and the dragon.

Then human beings will come to understand these things, to reflect on them with understanding, and they will bring mind and feeling and will to meet the autumn in the course of the year. Then, at the beginning of autumn, at the Michael festival, the picture of Michael with the dragon will confront us as a stark challenge, a strong spur to action, which must work on us in the midst of the events of our times. And then we shall understand how it points symptomatically to something in which the whole destiny — perhaps indeed the tragedy — of our epoch is being played out.

During the last three or four centuries we have developed a magnificent natural science and a far-reaching technology based on the most widely distributed material to be found on earth. We have learnt to make out of *iron* nearly all the most essential and important things produced by mankind in a materialistic age. In our locomotives, our factories, on all sides we see how we have built up this whole civilization on iron, or on steel, which is only iron transformed. And all the uses to which iron is put are a symptomatic indication of how we have built our whole life and outlook out of matter, and want to go on doing so. That is, however, a downward-leading path. We can rescue ourselves from its impending dangers only if we start to spiritualize life in this very domain; if we penetrate through our environment to the spiritual, if we turn from the iron which is used for making engines and look up again to the meteoric iron which showers down from the cosmos to the earth and is the outer material from which the power of Michael is forged. Human beings must come to see the great significance of the following words: 'Here on earth, in this epoch of materialism, you have made use of iron in accordance with the insight gained from your observation of matter. Now, just as you must transform your vision of matter through the further development of natural science into spiritual science, so must you rise from your former idea of iron to an understanding of meteoric iron, the iron of Michael's sword. And what you do there will make you whole. This is contained in the words:

O Man,
You shape it (*iron*) to your service,
You display it (*iron*) according to the value of its
substance
In many of your products.
Yet it will only make you whole
When it reveals to you
The exalted dominion of its spirit.

That is, the exalted dominion of Michael, with the sword
that will weld itself together in cosmic space out of meteoric
iron when our materialistic civilization becomes capable of
spiritualizing the power of iron into the power of Michael-
iron, which gives us self-consciousness in place of mere
nature-consciousness.

You have seen that precisely the most important demand
of our time, the Michael-demand, is implicit in this
inscription, this script contained in the astral light.

Lecture 2

THE CHRISTMAS IMAGINATION

Yesterday the picture of Michael battling with the dragon stood before us, revealed through an inner understanding of the course of the year. And art can really be nothing else than a reflection of what human beings feel in relation to the universe. This is, of course, possible at various levels and from various standpoints, but on the whole a work of art will only be genuine if we get the feeling that it opens up our soul to the secrets of the universe.

Today, in the same spirit that led us to the culminating picture of Michael and the dragon, we will carry further our study of the seasons of the year.

We know from yesterday's lecture that when autumn draws on a kind of inbreathing of the earth, a spiritual inbreathing, occurs, and the elemental beings are drawn back into the bosom of the earth. Those that went out in the height of summer and turned back at Michaelmas are drawn further and further in until, in the depths of winter, they are united most closely with the earth.

Now we must form the picture that in winter the earth is most of all self-contained, enclosed in itself. It has drawn back everything of a spiritual nature which it had allowed to stream out from itself during the summer. Hence in the depths of winter the earth is more earthly, more truly itself, than at any other time. And while for our further studies we must keep firmly in view this winter character of the earth, we must of course not forget that when winter prevails over half the earth the other half is experiencing summer. This is a fact we must keep in the background of our minds. But just now we are concerned with the coming of winter to one part of the earth. It is then that the earth unfolds its own nature in the deepest sense—the nature that makes it truly earth.

Let us now look at this earth of ours. It has a solid core hidden below its visible outer surface which, in turn, is largely covered with water, the hydrosphere. The continents are only floating, as it were, in this great watery expanse. And we can picture the hydrosphere as extending up into the atmosphere, for the atmosphere is always permeated by a watery element. Certainly this is much thinner than the water of the sea and the rivers, but there is no definite boundary in the atmosphere where the watery element comes to an end. Hence if we are to show schematically what the earth is like in this respect we should have, first, a solid core in the centre [see Plate 1]. Around it we have the watery regions [blue]. I must of course indicate the jutting up of the continents; they will have to be exaggerated, for they should really be no more prominent than the irregularities on the skin of an orange. Then I must put in the hydrosphere, this watery part of the atmosphere all round the earth. Let us look at this picture [blue] and ask ourselves what it really represents. It is not something made up entirely out of itself; it is water shaped by the whole cosmos. This body of air and water is spherical because the cosmos extends round it as a sphere on all sides. And this means that strong forces play in on the earth as a whole.

The effect is that if we were to look at the earth from some other planet it would appear to us as a great water drop in the cosmos. There would be all sorts of prominences on it—the continents, which would be rather differently coloured—but as a whole it would appear to us as a great water drop in the midst of the universe.

Let us now consider this from a cosmic standpoint. What is this great water drop? It is something which takes its shape from its whole cosmic environment.

If one approaches the matter from a spiritual-scientific

point of view, bringing Imagination and Inspiration to bear on it, one comes to know what this water drop really is. It is nothing but a gigantic drop of quicksilver, but the quicksilver is present in an extraordinarily rarefied condition.

The possibility of these high rarefactions has been demonstrated by the work of Frau Dr Kolisko. At our Biological Institute in Stuttgart the attempt has been made for the first time to put this on a scientific basis. It has been possible to make dilutions of substances up to one part in a trillion, in fact to establish precisely the effects which such high dilutions of particular substances can have. Hitherto, in homoeopathy, this has been merely a matter of belief; now it has been raised to the level of exact science. The graphs which have been drawn leave no doubt today that the effects of the smallest particles follow a rhythmical course. I will not go into details; the work has been published and these findings can now be verified. Here I wish only to point out that even in the earthly realm the effects of enormous dilutions must be reckoned with.

Here we are concerned with something of which we can say, when we use it on a small scale: this is water. We can draw water from a river or a well and use it as water. Yes, it is water, but there is no water that consists solely of hydrogen and oxygen. It would be absurd for anyone to suppose that water consists of hydrogen and oxygen only. In the case of mineral waters and suchlike it is of course obvious that something else is present. But no water anywhere is composed solely of hydrogen and oxygen; that is only a first approximation. All water, wherever it appears, is permeated with something else. Essentially, the whole water mass of the earth is quicksilver for the universe. Only the small quantities we use are water for us. For the universe this water is not water but quicksilver.

Hence we can say, first of all, that in so far as we are considering the hydrosphere in relation to water we have to do with a drop of quicksilver in the cosmos. Embedded as it were in this drop of quicksilver, naturally, are mineral substances — in brief, all the earthly substances. They represent the solid mass of the earth, and they tend to assume their own special forms. Thus in the structure as a whole we observe quicksilver. Ordinary metallic quicksilver, one might say, is only the symbol produced by nature for the general activity of quicksilver, leading quite definitely to a spherical form. Embedded in the whole sphere are the metallic crystals, with the manifold variety of their own distinctive forms. Hence we have before us this formation of earth, water, air; and its tendency, as I have said, is to assume a spherical form, with individual crystal forms within it [Plate 1].

Even if we single out the air [dark red] which surrounds the earth as its atmosphere, we can never speak simply of air, for the air always has a tendency to contain warmth in some degree: the air is permeated with warmth [violet]. Thus we must add this fourth element, warmth, which permeates the air.

Now this warmth which comes into the air from above carries pre-eminently within it the sulphur process imparted to it from the cosmos. And to the sulphur process is added the mercurial process as I have described in connection with the hydrosphere. Thus we have: air-warmth, the sulphur process; water-air, the mercurial process.

If we now turn towards the inner part of the earth we come to the acid formation process and especially to the salt process, for the salts derive from the acids; and this is what the earth really wants to be. Hence when we look up into the cosmos we are really looking at the sulphur process. When we consider the tendency of the earth to form itself into a cosmic water drop we are really looking at the mercurial process. And if we turn our gaze to the solid earth underfoot, which in spring gives rise to all that we see as growing, sprouting life, we are looking at the salt process.

This salt process is all-important for springtime life and

growth. For the roots of plants, in forming themselves out of the seeds, depend for their whole growth on their relation to the salt formations in the soil. It is these salt formations – in the widest sense of the term – the deposit formations within the crust of the earth, which give substance to the roots and enable them to act as the earthly foundation of plant life.

Thus in turning back to the earth we encounter the salt process. This is what the earth makes of itself in the depths of winter, whereas in summer there is much more inter-mingling. For in summer the air is shot through with sul-phurizing processes, which indeed occur also in lightning and thunder; they penetrate far down, so that the whole course of the season is sulphurized. Then we come to Michaelmas, to the time when the sulphur process is driven back by meteoric iron, as I told you yesterday. During summer, too, the salt process mingles with the atmosphere, for the growing plants carry the salts up through their leaves and blossoms right up into the seeds. Naturally we find the salt widely distributed in the plant. They ethere-alize themselves in the essential oils, and so on; they approach the sulphurizing process. The salts are carried up through the plants; they stream out and become part of the being of the atmosphere.

In high summer, accordingly, we have a mingling of the mercurial element, always present in the earth, with the sulphurizing and salt forming elements. If at this season we stand here on earth our head actually projects into a mix-ture of sulphur, mercury and salt; while the arrival of midwinter means that each of these three principles reverts to its own inner condition. The salts are drawn back into the inner part of the earth, and the tendency for the hydro-sphere to assume a spherical shape reasserts itself – imaged in winter by the snow mantle that covers parts of the earth. The sulphur process withdraws, so that there is no parti-cular occasion to observe it. In place of it something else comes to the fore during the midwinter season.

The plants have developed from spring until autumn, finally concentrating themselves in their seeds. What is this seeding process? When plants run to seed they are doing what we are constantly doing in a dull human way when we use plants for food. We cook them. Now the development of a plant to blossom and then to seed production is nature's cookery; it encounters the sulphur process. The plants grow up and out into the sulphur process. They are most strongly sulphurized when summer is at its height. When autumn draws on, this combustion process comes to an end.

In the organic realm, of course, everything is different from the processes we observe in their coarse inorganic form, but the outcome of every combustion process is ash. And in addition to the salt formation, which comes from quite another quarter and is needed within the earth, we must add all that falls to the earth from the blossoming and seeding of plants as a result of the cooking or combustion process. This falling of ash — just as ash falls in our stoves — plays a great role, which is usually overlooked. For in the course of seed formation — which is fundamentally a combustion process — the seed nature is continually showering down on the earth, so that from October onwards the earth is quite impregnated with this form of ash.

If therefore we observe the earth in the depths of winter, we have first the internal tendency to salt formation. Besides this we have the mercurial shaping process in its most strongly marked form. And while in high summer we have to pay attention to the sulphurizing process in the cosmos outside the earth, in winter we now have the ash-forming process.

So you see, its culmination at Christmas is prepared in advance from Michaelmas onwards. The earth is gradually more and more consolidated, so that in midwinter it becomes really a cosmic body expressing itself in mercurial formation, salt formation, ash formation. What does this signify for the cosmos?

Now, if we can suppose that a flea, let us say, were to become an anatomist and were to study a bone, it would have in front of it minute pieces of bone, because the flea itself is so small and it would be examining the bone from a flea's perspective. The flea would then discover that in the bone there is phosphate of lime in an amorphous condition, with carbonic acid, lime and so forth. But our flea anatomist would never come to the point of realizing that the fragment of the bone is a small part only of a complete skeleton. Certainly the flea jumps, but in studying the tiny piece of bone he would never get beyond it. Similarly, it would not help a human geologist or mineralogist to be able to jump about like a gigantic earth flea. In studying the mountain ranges of the earth, which in their totality represent a skeleton, he would still be working on a minute scale. The flea would never come to describing the skeleton as a whole; he would hack out a tiny piece with his tiny hammer. Suppose this were a tiny piece of collar bone. Nothing in the constituents of the little piece, carbonate of lime, phosphate of lime, and so on, would reveal to the flea that it belonged to a collar bone, still less that it was part of a complete skeleton. The flea would have hacked off a tiny piece and would then describe it from his own flea standpoint, just as a human being describes the earth when somewhere — let us say in the Dornach hills — he has hacked out a bit of Jura limestone. Then he describes this bit, and works up his findings into mineralogy, geology, and so on. It is still the same flea standpoint, though on a larger scale.

In this way we cannot arrive at the truth. We need to recognize that the earth is a single whole, most firmly consolidated during winter through its salt formation, its mercurial formation and its ash formation. Let us then ask what the whole nature of the earth signifies when we look at it not from the flea's point of view, but in relation to the cosmos.

We will first consider salt formation, taking this in the

widest sense to connote a physical deposit, exemplified in the way ordinary cooking salt, dissolved in a glass of water, will separate out as a deposit on the bottom of the glass. (I will not go into the chemical side of this, though the result would be the same if I did.) Now a salt deposit of this kind has the characteristic of being porous, as it were, to the spirit. Where there is a salt deposit the spiritual element has a clear field of entry. In midwinter, accordingly, when the earth consolidates itself through salt formation, the effect is first of all that the elemental beings who are united with the earth have, one might say, an agreeable abode within. But spiritual elements of another kind are also drawn in from the cosmos, and are able to dwell in the salt crust which lies immediately below the earth's surface. Here, in this salt crust, the moon forces are particularly active — I mean the remains of those moon forces which were left behind, as I have often mentioned, when the moon separated from the earth.

These moon forces are active in the earth chiefly because of the salt present in it. So in winter — beneath the snow cover which strives in one direction, one might say towards the quicksilver form, and in the other direction passes down into the salt element — we have the solid earth substance, the salt, permeated with spirituality. In winter the earth does indeed become spiritual in itself through the con-solidating influence, especially, of its salt content.

Now water — that is, cosmic quicksilver — has the inner tendency to shape itself spherically. We can see this inner tendency everywhere. And because of this the earth in midwinter is enabled not only to solidify through its salt content and to permeate the salt with spirit, but also to vivify the spiritualized substance and to lead it over into the realm of life. In winter the whole surface of the earth is reinvigorated. The quicksilver principle, working into the spiritualized salt, activates everywhere this tendency towards new life. Below the earth's surface, in winter, there is a tremendous re-enlivening of the earth's capacity to produce life.

This life, however, would become a moon life, for it is chiefly the moon forces that are active in it. But because ash falls down from the seeds of plants, so that everything I have just described is impregnated with ash, something is present which keeps the whole process under the control of the earth.

The plants have striven upwards into the sulphur process, and out of this process the ash has descended. This is what draws the plant back to earth after it has striven up into the etheric-spiritual. So in the depths of winter we have on the earth's surface not only the tendency to absorb the spirit and to reinvigorate itself, but also the tendency to transform what is of a moon nature into earth nature. Through the remains of the fallen ash the moon is compelled to promote earthly life, not moon life.

Now let us turn from the earth's surface and look at the air formation that surrounds the earth. For the air, it is of the utmost importance always, but especially in midwinter, that the sun radiates warmth and light through it—though the light is less relevant to our immediate considerations.

You see, science treats things always in isolation, as in reality they never are. Air, we are told, consists of oxygen and nitrogen and other elements. But in fact this is not so; the air is not made up merely of oxygen and nitrogen, for it is always rayed through by the sun. That is the reality; air is always permeated in the daytime by the activity of the sun. And what does this activity signify? It signifies that the air up above is always seeking to tear itself away from the earth. If salt formation, mercurial formation and ash formation were alone active, then nothing but earth activity would be there. But up above, because the activities striving upwards from the earth are taken up into the activity of sun and air, earth activity is transmuted into cosmic activity. The power to work on its own accord in the realm of life and spirit is taken away from the earth. The sun makes its power felt in everything that grows and sprouts upwards from the earth. And so, in a certain region above the earth, a quite special tendency is apparent to spiritual vision [Plate 1]. On the earth itself everything seeks to become spherical [dark red]; in this upper region the sphere is continually impelled to flatten out into a plane [reddish]. Naturally it will tend to resume its spherical shape, but up there the spherical is always inclined to flatten out. The upper influences would really like to break up the earth, to disintegrate it, so that everything might become a flat surface, spread out there in the cosmos.

If this were to come about the earth's activities would disappear completely, and up above we should have a kind of air in which the stars would be active. This is very plainly expressed in man himself. What do we get, as human beings, from the sun-filled air above? We breathe it in, and because of this the activity of the sun extends right into us, downwards in a sense but chiefly upwards. Through our head we are continually drawn away from the influences of the earth, and on this account our head is enabled to participate in the whole cosmos. Our head would really always like to go out into the region where the plane prevails. If our head belonged only to the earth, especially in wintertime, our whole experience of thinking would be different. We should then have the feeling that all our thoughts wished to take a rounded shape. In fact they do not; they have a certain lightness, adaptability, fluidity, and this we owe to the characteristic incursion of the activity of the sun.

Here we have the second tendency; here the sun activity intervenes in earthly activity. But this is at its weakest in winter. If we were to go still further out something else would come into the picture. Then we should no longer have to do with the activity of the sun but only with the activity of the stars, for the stars in their turn have a great influence on our head. Inasmuch as the sun gives us back to the cosmos, as it were, the stars have their own deeply penetrating influence on our head, and so on the whole formation of the human organism.

But now I must tell you that what I have just been describing no longer holds good today, for in a certain way human beings have emancipated themselves, in their development and their whole evolution, from the earth's activities. If we were to go back to the ancient Lemurian time, or especially to the Polarian time that preceded it, we should find a quite different state of affairs. We should observe that everything that occurred on the earth had a great influence on the human organism. You will indeed have gathered this from the account of the evolution of the earth given in my *Occult Science*. In those early times we should find mankind placed in the very midst of the activities I have described. Tomorrow I will describe how human beings have emancipated themselves from all this; today I will speak as though we were still fully involved in it. And here we come to something that to the modern mind will seem highly paradoxical.

We can ask the question: What does a mother become when she is beginning to develop a new human being within her? At first—after all that has first to happen in order that a new human being may come into existence on earth—it is the salt-forming moon forces which chiefly influence the female organism at that time. So we can say that while a woman is in other respects and in general a human being, the salt-forming moon forces then have the strongest influence on her. We can put this in spiritual scientific terms by saying: The woman becomes moon, just as the earth—especially just below its surface— becomes moon when Christmas approaches.

So it is not the earth only which becomes mostly moon when midwinter prevails; this tendency of the earth to become moon occurs again, in like manner, when a woman prepares herself to receive a new human being. And precisely because of this the sun influence on her becomes different, just as it is different in midwinter compared with midsummer. And the formation in the woman of the new human being stands wholly under the influence of the sun. It is because the woman takes up the moon activities, the salt activities, so strongly into herself that she becomes able to secrete the sun activities separately. In ordinary life the sun activities are taken up by the human organism through the heart and from there spread out over the whole organism. But directly a woman prepares herself to bring forth a new human being the sun activities are concentrated on the forming of this new life. Thus we can say schematically: The woman becomes moon so that she can take up the sun activities into herself; and the new human being, existing first as an embryo, is in this sense wholly sun activity. The embryo is enabled to come into being through the concentration of sun activities.

The old instinctive clairvoyance knew this in its own way. At one time in ancient Europe a remarkable idea prevailed. It was thought that before a newborn child had taken any earthly nourishment it was a quite different being from what it became after imbibing its first drop of milk. That was the old German belief. For these people had an instinctive feeling that the newborn infant was a sun being, and that through the first earthly nourishment it received it became a creature of earth. Hence the newborn infant did not at first belong to the earth at all. Again, according to occult laws which I might touch on at some other time, old Germanic custom gave the father—at whose feet the child was always laid directly it was born—the right either to let it grow or to destroy it; for it was not yet a creature of earth. If it had taken one single drop of milk he no longer had the right to destroy it. It would then have to remain an earth creature, because it had been ordained by nature, by the world, by the cosmos, to be one. In such old customs there lives something of very deep significance.

Here indeed is the basis of the saying 'The child is of the sun'. So it is possible now to look on the woman who has borne the child as a being who is in the deepest sense related to all earthly processes. For the earth prepares itself in midwinter through the salt element—that is, the moon element—so that it may be best able to receive the sun element. The earth then reaches out beyond the sun element to the heavens, to which also the human head belongs.

Hence we can say something like this. In order to bring the essence of Christmas rightly before our souls let us transpose ourselves into the being of man. The celebration of Christmas expresses the coming to birth of the Jesus-child who is ordained to receive the Christ into himself. Let us look closely at this. If we look at the figure of Mary we are bound to see that her head reflects something heavenly in its whole appearance, its whole expression. We must then indicate that Mary is preparing to take into herself the sun, the child, the sun as it rays through the encircling air. And then we can see in the form of Mary the moon-earthly element.

Now imagine how this could be portrayed. First we have the moon-earth element, spreading out below the earth's surface. Then, going out into the great spaces, we find a raying forth from man into the cosmos, and this could be shown as a heavenly earth-star radiance, sent out by the earth into the cosmos. The head of Mary is like a radiant star, which means that her whole countenance and bearing must give expression to this star-radiant quality [Plate 2].

If we then turn to the chest part we come to the breathing process, to the sun element, the child, forming itself out of the clouds in the atmosphere, shot through by the rays of the sun.

Further down we come to the moonlike, salt-forming forces, given outward expression by bringing the limbs into dynamic relation with the earth and letting them arise out of the salt and the moon elements in the earth. Here we have the earth in so far as it is inwardly transfigured by the moon. All this would really have to be shown through a kind of rainbow colouring. For if we were to look from the cosmos towards the earth, through the shining of the stars, it would be as though the earth were wishing to shine inwardly, beneath its surface, in rainbow colours. On the earth we have something related to the earth forces, to gravity and to the formation of the limbs, which can be expressed only through the garment which follows the earth forces in its folds. So we should have the garment down below, in relation to the earth forces. Then we should have to portray, a little higher up, that which gives expression to the earth-moon element. We could even picture the moon, if we wished to symbolize, but the moon element is clearly expressed in the configuration of the earth. Higher up still we must bring in that which issues from the moon element. We see how the clouds are filled with many human heads, pressing downwards; one of them is condensed into the sun resting on Mary's arm: the Jesus-child. And all this must be completed, in an upward direction, through the star radiance expressed in the countenance of Mary.

If we understand how the depths of winter show us the connection of the cosmos with the human being, with the human being who takes up the birth forces in the earth, then the only possible way of presenting the woman is in this form: formed out of the clouds, endowed with the forces of the earth; with the moon forces below, with the sun forces in the middle, and above, towards the head, with the forces of the stars. The picture of Mary with the little Jesus-child arises out of the cosmos itself.

If we understand the cosmos in autumn, then so as to represent all its formative forces in a picture we come by necessity to an artistic portrayal of Michael and the dragon, as I indicated yesterday. In the same way, everything we feel at Christmas-time flows together into the picture of

Mary and the child—that picture which hovered so often before artists in earlier times, especially in the first Christian centuries, and of which the after-effects have been preserved in Raphael's *Sistine Madonna*.

The *Sistine Madonna* was born out of the deep instinctive knowledge of nature and the spirit which prevailed in ancient times. For it is an Imagination, something which must in fact come to a person who transposes his inner vision into the secrets of Christmas in such a way that they become for him a living picture.

Hence we can say: The course of the seasons must appear to the inner vision in clear and glorious Imaginations. If one goes out with one's whole being into the world's surroundings, the approach of autumn becomes the glorious Imagination of Michael's fight with the dragon. Just as the dragon can be represented only in a sulphurous form—born out of the sulphur clouds—and just as the sword of Michael appears when we think of the meteoric iron as concentrated in the sword and blended with it, so out of all that we can feel at Christmas-time there arises the picture of Mary the mother, the folds of her robe following the forces of the earth, while in the region of the chest—even these details are apparent in the painting—her garment has to be inwardly rounded, taking on the quicksilver form, so that here one has a feeling of inward enclosure. Here the sun forces can find entry, and the innocent Jesus-child, who must be thought of as having not yet received any earthly nourishment, is the sun activity resting on Mary's arm, with the radiance of the stars above. This is how we have to represent the head and eyes of Mary, as though a light were shining out from within them towards humanity. And the Jesus-child in Mary's arms must appear as though emerging from the rounded cloud shapes, tender and lovable, inwardly sheltered; and then the garment, subject to earthly gravity, expressing what the force of earthly gravity can become [Plate 2].

All this is best rendered in colours. Then we have the picture which will shine out for us as a cosmic Imagination at Christmas-time — a picture we can live with until Easter, when out of cosmic relationships once again an Easter Imagination can arise; we shall speak of it tomorrow.

You will see from this that art is drawn from the interplay of the heavens and the earth. True art is what human beings experience in conjunction with the body, soul and spirit of the cosmos as it reveals itself to them in magnificent Imaginations. So, to represent all that is involved in the inner struggle for the development of self-consciousness out of nature-consciousness, nothing will do but the grand picture of Michael's fight with the dragon; and to bring before us everything that can work from nature into our souls during the midwinter season, we have an artistic, imaginative expression in the picture of the mother and the child.

To observe the course of the seasons is to follow the great cosmic artist, so that what the heavens imprint on the earth is brought to life again in powerful pictures — pictures that grow into realities in the human heart.

Thus the course of the year can reveal itself to us in four Imaginations: the Michael Imagination, the Mary Imagination and — as we shall see later on — the Easter Imagination and the St John Imagination.

Lecture 3

THE EASTER IMAGINATION

We must realize clearly how it is that in the depths of winter the earth, in relation to the cosmos, actually becomes a self-enclosed being. During the winter the earth's whole nature is concentrated, it becomes wholly earth. In high summer — to add this contrast for the sake of clarity — the earth is open to the cosmos, lives with the cosmos. And in between, during spring and autumn, there is always a balance between these extremes.

All this has the deepest significance for the earth's whole life. Naturally, what I shall be saying applies only to that part of the earth's surface where a corresponding transition from winter to spring takes place.

Let us start, as we have always done in these lectures, by considering the purely material aspect. We shall look at the salt deposits which we have had to treat as the most important factor in wintertime. We shall study this first in the limestone deposits, which are indeed of the utmost importance for the whole being of the earth.

You need only go out-of-doors here, where we are surrounded everywhere by the Jura limestone, and you will have around you all that I shall begin with today. Ordinary observation is so superficial that for most people limestone is simply limestone, and outwardly there really is no perceptible difference between winter limestone and spring limestone. But this failure to distinguish between them comes from the standpoint which yesterday I called the flea-standpoint. The metamorphoses of limestone appear only when we look deeper into the cosmos, as it were. Then we find a subtle difference between winter limestone and spring limestone, and it is precisely this which makes limestone the most important of all deposits in the soil. After all the various considerations we have gone into here, and since we know that soul and spirit are to be found everywhere, we can allow ourselves to speak of all such substance as vivified, ensouled beings. Thus we can say that winter limestone is a being content within itself.

If we penetrate with Intuition into the being of winter limestone, as Intuition is described in my book *Knowledge of Higher Worlds* — we find it permeated throughout with the most diverse spirituality, made up of the elemental beings who dwell in the earth. But the limestone is as it were contented, as a human head may be when it has solved an important problem and feels happy to have the thoughts which point to the solution. We perceive — for Intuition always embraces feeling — an inner contentment in the whole neighbourhood of the limestone formations during the winter season.

If we were to swim under water, we should perceive water everywhere; and similarly, if we move spiritually through the process of limestone formation, we perceive this winter contentment on all sides. It expresses itself as an inner permeation of the winter limestone by mobile, ever-changing forms — living, spiritual forms which appear as Imaginations.

When spring approaches, however, and especially when March comes, the limestone becomes — we may say — dull in respect of its spiritual qualities. It loses them, for, as you know from previous accounts, the elemental beings now take their way, through a kind of cosmic-spiritual exhalation, into the cosmos. The limestone's spiritual thinking qualities are dulled, but the remarkable thing is that it becomes full of eager desire. It develops a kind of inner vitality. A subtle living energy arises increasingly in the limestone, becoming steadily more active as spring draws on, and even more so towards summer, as the plants shoot up.

These things are naturally not apparent in a crude outward form, but in a subtle, intimate way they do occur. The growing plants draw water and carbonic acid from the limestone in the soil. But this very loss signifies for the limestone an inner access of living activity, and it acquires on this account an extraordinary power of attraction for the ahrimanic beings. Whenever spring approaches their hopes revive. Apart from this, they have nothing particular to hope for from the realm of outer nature, because they are really able to pursue their activities only within human beings, namely, in their animal nature. But when spring draws near the impression which the spring limestone makes on them gives them the idea that after all they will be able to spread their dragon-nature through nature at large. Finding the spring limestone full of life, they hope to be able to draw in also the astral element from the cosmos in order to ensoul the limestone — to permeate it with soul. So, when March is near, a truly clairvoyant observer of nature can witness a remarkable drama. He sees how everywhere the hopes of the ahrimanic beings play over the earth like an astral wind, and how the ahrimanic beings strive with all their might to call down an astral rain, as it were. If they were to succeed, then in the summer this astral rain would transform the earth into an ensouled being — or at least partly, as far as the limestone extends. And then, in autumn, the earth would feel pain at every footfall on its surface.

This endeavour, this illusion, lays hold of the ahrimanic beings every spring, and every spring it is brought to nothing. From a human standpoint, one might say, surely by now the ahrimanic beings must have become clever enough to renounce these hopes. But the world is not just as human beings imagine it to be. The fact is that every spring the ahrimanic beings have new hope of being able to transform the earth into an ensouled, living being, through an astral rain from above, and every year their illusions are shattered.

But human beings are not free from danger in the midst of these illusions. They consume the nature products which flourish in this atmosphere of hopes and illusions; and it is naive to suppose that the bread we eat is merely grain, ground and baked. For within it are the illusions and hopes of the ahrimanic beings. In outer nature these hopes are shattered, but the ahrimanic beings long all the more to achieve their aim in human beings who already have a soul. Thus every spring human beings are in danger of falling victim — in subtle intimate ways — to the ahrimanic beings. In spring they are much more exposed to all the ahrimanic workings in the cosmos than they are during other times of the year.

But now, if we direct our gaze upwards, to where the elemental beings of the earth ascend, where they unite themselves with the cloud formations and acquire an inner activity which is subject to planetary life, something else can be seen. As March approaches, and down below the ahrimanic beings are at work, the elemental beings — who are wholly spiritual, immaterial, although they live within the material earth — are transported up into the region of vapour, air and warmth. And all that goes on up there among the active elemental beings is permeated by luciferic beings. Just as the ahrimanic beings nourish their hopes and experience their illusions down below, so the luciferic beings experience their hopes and illusions up above.

If we look more closely at the ahrimanic beings we find they are of etheric nature. And it is impossible for these beings, who are really those cast down by Michael, to develop in any other way than by trying to gain domination over the earth through the life and desire that fill the limestone in spring.

The luciferic beings up above stream through and permeate all the activities that have risen up from the earth. They are of a purely astral nature. Through everything that begins to strive upwards in spring they gain the hope of being able to permeate their astral nature with the etheric, and to call forth from the earth an etheric sheath in which they could then take up their habitation.

Hence we can say: The ahrimanic beings try to ensoul the earth with astrality [Plate 3, reddish]; the luciferic beings try to take up the etheric into their own being [blue with yellow].

When in spring the plants begin to sprout they draw in and assimilate carbon dioxide. Hence the carbon dioxide is active in a higher region than it is in winter; it rises into the realm of the plants and there it is drawn towards the luciferic beings. While the ahrimanic beings try to ensoul the living limestone with a kind of astral rain, the luciferic beings try to raise up a sort of carbon dioxide mist or vapour from the earth [Plate 3, blue, yellow]. If they were to succeed, human beings on earth would no longer be able to breathe. The luciferic beings would draw up all mankind's etheric nature, which is not dependent on physical breathing, and by uniting themselves with it they would be able to become etheric beings, whereas they are now only astral beings. And then, with the extinction of all human and animal life on earth, up above there would be a sheath of etheric angel beings. That is what the luciferic beings strive and hope for when the end of March approaches. They hope to change the whole earth into a delicate shell of this kind, wherein, densified through the etheric nature of mankind, they could carry on their own existence.

If the ahrimanic beings could realize their hopes the whole of humanity would gradually be dissolved into the earth; the earth would absorb them. Finally — and that is Ahriman's intention — the earth would become a single great entity in which all human beings would be merged — they would be united with it. But the transition to this union with the earth would consist in human beings in their whole organism becoming more and more like the living limestone. They would blend the living limestone with their organism and become more and more calcified. In this way they would transmute their bodily form into one that looked quite different — a sclerotic form with something like bat's wings and a head like this [Plate 4]. This form would then be able to merge gradually into the earthly element, so that the whole earth, according to the ahrimanic idea, would become a living earth being.

If the luciferic beings, on the other hand, could absorb the etheric nature of humanity, and thus condense themselves from an astral to an etheric condition, then they would assume an etheric form in which the lower parts of the human organism would be more or less absent and the upper part would be transformed. The body would be formed of earth vapour [Plate 4, blue], developed only as far down as the chest, with an idealized human head [red]. And the peculiar thing is that this being would have wings, born as it were out of clouds [yellow]. In front, these wings would concentrate into a sort of enlarged larynx; at the sides they would concentrate into ears, organs of hearing, which again would be connected with the larynx.

You see, I tried to represent the sclerotic form through the figure of Ahriman in the painting in the dome of the Goetheanum and sculpturally in the wood carving of the Group. Similarly, the luciferic shape, created out of earth vapour and cloud masses, as it would be if it could take up the etheric from the earth, is represented there.[*]

Thus the two human extremes are written into the life of the earth itself: first, the extreme that human beings would come to if, under the influence of Ahriman, they were to

---

[*] The central motif (painted from a sketch by Rudolf Steiner) in the small dome of the First Goetheanum, and in Rudolf Steiner's wood carving of the *Representative of Humanity*.

take up the living limestone and thereby become gradually one with the earth, dissolved into the whole living, sentient earth. That is one extreme. The other extreme is what human beings would come to if the luciferic beings were to succeed in causing a vapour of carbonic acid to rise from below, so that breathing would be extinguished and physical humanity would disappear, while the human etheric bodies would be united with the astrality of the luciferic angel being above.

Again we can say: These are the hopes, the illusions, of the luciferic beings. Anyone who looks out as a seer into the great spaces of the cosmos does not see in the moving clouds, as in Shakespeare's play, a shape which looks first like a camel and then like something else. When March comes he sees in the clouds the dynamic striving forces of the luciferic beings who would like to create out of the earth a luciferic sheath. Mankind sways between these two extremes. The desire of both the luciferic and the ahrimanic beings is to obliterate humanity as it exists today.

These various activities are made manifest within the life of the earth. The hopes of the luciferic beings are shattered once more every spring, but they work on in human beings. And in springtime, while on the one hand they are exposed to the ahrimanic forces, they are also exposed more and more — and right on through the summer — to the luciferic beings.

These forces, certainly, work in so subtle a way that they are noticed today only by someone who is spiritually sensitive and can really live with the course of events in the cosmos round the year. But in earlier times, even in the later Atlantean period, all this had great significance.

In those earlier times, for example, human reproduction was bound up with the seasons. Conception could occur only in the spring, when the forces were active in the way I have described, and births could therefore take place only towards the end of the year. The life of the earth was thus bound up in a wholesome way with human life.[*]

Now a principle of the luciferic beings is to set free everything on earth, including conception and birth. That human beings can be born at any time of the year came about in earlier times through the luciferic influence which frees mankind from the earth. This has now become an integral part of human freedom; luciferic forces are actually at work there. Next time I will speak of influences that are still active, but today I wished to show you how in earlier times the aims of the luciferic beings were actually achieved, up to a certain point. Otherwise, human beings could have been born only in winter.

As against this, the ahrimanic beings try with all their might to draw man back into connection with the earth. And since the luciferic beings had this great influence in the past, the ahrimanic beings have a prospect of at least partly achieving their purpose of binding man to the earth by merging his mind and disposition with the earthly element and turning him into a complete materialist. They would like to make his capacity to think and feel depend entirely on the food he digests. This ahrimanic influence bears particularly on our own epoch, and will get stronger and stronger.

If, therefore, we look back in time, we come to something accomplished by the luciferic beings and bequeathed to us. If we look forward towards the end of the earth, we see humanity faced with the threatening prospect that the ahrimanic beings, since they cannot actually dissolve humanity into the earth, will contrive at least to harden human beings so that they become crude materialists,

---

[*] See the lecture entitled 'Christmas at a Time of Grievous Destiny', given in Basle, 21 December 1916. Published in *Festivals and Their Meaning*, Rudolf Steiner Press, 1996.

thinking and feeling only what material substance thinks and feels in them.

The luciferic beings accomplished their work in freeing humanity from nature, in the way I have described, at a time when human beings themselves had as yet no freedom. Freedom has not arisen through human resolve or in an abstract way, as the usual account suggests, but because natural processes, such as the timing of births, have come under human control. That freedom has arisen at all is because of what has taken place in the realm of natural processes such as this. When in earlier times it became obvious that children could be born at any season, this brought a feeling of freedom into the soul and spirit of man. These are the facts. They depend far more on the cosmos than is commonly imagined.

But now that human beings have advanced in freedom, they should use their freedom to banish the threatening danger that Ahriman will fetter them to the earth. For in the perspective of the future this threat stands before us. And here we see how into earth evolution there came an objective fact: the Mystery of Golgotha. Although the Mystery of Golgotha had indeed to enter as a once-and-for-all event into the history of the earth, it is in a sense renewed for human beings each year. We can learn to feel how the luciferic force up above would like to suffocate physical humanity in carbon dioxide vapour, while down below the ahrimanic forces would like to vivify the limestone masses of the earth with an astral rain, so that humanity itself would be calcified and reduced to limestone. But then, for a person who can see these things, there arises between the luciferic and the ahrimanic forces the figure of Christ: the Christ who, freeing Himself from the weight of matter, has Ahriman under His feet; who is wresting Himself free from the ahrimanic and taking no heed of it because He is overcoming it, as we have shown here in painting and sculpture. And here is shown also how the Christ is overcoming the force that seeks to draw the upper part of the human being away from the earth. The head of the Christ figure, the conqueror of Ahriman, appears with a countenance, a look and a bearing wrested from the dissolvent forces of Lucifer. The luciferic power drawn into the earthly realm and held there, such is the form of the Christ as He appears every year in spring. That is how we must picture Him: standing on the earth, which Ahriman seeks to make his own; victorious over death; ascending from the grave as the Risen One to the transfiguration which comes from carrying over the luciferic element into the earthly beauty of the countenance of Christ.

Thus the Risen Christ in His Resurrection form appears before our eyes, between the luciferic and the ahrimanic forms, as the Easter picture; the Risen Christ, with luciferic powers hovering above and the ahrimanic powers under his feet.

This cosmic Imagination comes before us as the Easter Imagination, just as we had the Virgin and Child as the Christmas Imagination in deep winter, and the Michael Imagination for the end of September. You will see how right it was to portray the Christ in the form you see here — a form born out of cosmic happenings in the course of the year. There is nothing arbitrary about this. Every look, every trait in the countenance, every flowing fold in the garment should be thought of as placing the Christ figure between the forms of Lucifer and Ahriman as the One who works in human evolution so that human beings may be wrested from the luciferic and ahrimanic powers at the very time, the time of Easter and spring, when they could most easily fall victim to them.

Here precisely in the figure of Christ we see again how nothing can be done properly out of the arbitrary fancies that are favoured in artistic circles today. If a person wishes to develop full freedom in the realm of art, he does not bind himself in a slavish, ahrimanic way to materials and models; he rises freely into spiritual heights and there he freely creates, for it is in spiritual heights that freedom can prevail. Then he will create out of a bluish-violet vapour a kind of chest form for the luciferic element and a form consisting of wings, larynx and ear as though emerging from reddish clouds, so that this form can appear in full reality as an image both of what these beings are in their astral nature and of the etheric guise they threaten to assume [Plate 4].

Place vividly before you these wings of Lucifer, working in the astral element and striving towards the etheric. You will find that because these wings are actually feeling about in cosmic spaces they are sensitive to all the secrets of force in the cosmos. Through their undulating movement, these wings, with their wavelike formation, are in touch with the mysterious, spiritual wave activities of the cosmos. And the experience brought by these waves passes through the ear formation into the inner nature of the luciferic being and is carried further there. The luciferic being grasps through his ear formation what he has sensed with his wings, and through the larynx—closely connected with the ear—this knowledge becomes the creative word that works and weaves in the forms of living beings.

If you picture a luciferic being of this kind, with his reddish-yellow formation of wings, ears and larynx, you will see in him the activity which is sensitive to the secrets of the cosmos through his wings experiencing these secrets through the inward continuation of his ear formation, and uttering them as creative word through the larynx, bound up with wings and ears in one organic whole.

Thus was Lucifer painted in the cupola, and thus is he represented in the sculptured Group which was intended to be the central point of our Goetheanum. Thus, in a certain sense, the Easter Mystery was to have stood at this central point. But a completion in some form will be necessary, if one is to grasp the whole idea. For all that can be seen as the threatening luciferic influence and the threatening ahrimanic influence belongs to the inner being of the nature forces and the direction they strive to take in spring and on into summer; and standing over against them is the healing principle that rays out from the Christ. However, a living feeling for all this will be attained when the whole architectural scheme is completed and what I have described exists in architectural and sculptural form, and when in the future it will be possible to present in front of the sculpture a living drama with two leading characters: the human being and Raphael.

It belongs to the character of this architecture and this sculpture that a kind of mystery play would have to be enacted with the human being and Raphael as chief characters—Raphael with the staff of Mercury and all that belongs to it. In living artistic work everything is a challenge, and fundamentally there is no sculpture and no architecture—if it is to be inwardly in accord with cosmic truth—which does not call for a presentation in the space surrounding it of the artistic action it embodies. At Easter this architecture and sculpture would call for a mystery play showing Raphael teaching man to see in what way the ahrimanic and luciferic forces make him ill, and how through the power of Raphael he can be led to perceive and recognize the healing principle, the great all-pervading therapy which lives in the Christ principle. If all this could be done—and the Goetheanum was designed for it all—then at Easter there would be, as well as a great many other things, a certain crowning of all that can flow into mankind from the ahrimanic and luciferic secrets.

You see, if we learn to recognize the springtime activity of the ahrimanic influence in the living limestone, through which a greedy endeavour is being made to take up the cosmic astral element, then we learn also to recognize the healing forces that reside in everything of a saltlike nature. The difference is not apparent in the coarser kind of activities, but it comes out in the healing ones. Thus we learn to know these healing influences by studying the workings of the ahrimanic beings in the salt deposits of the earth. For whatever is permeated by ahrimanic influences during *one* season of the year—we will go into this in greater detail next time—is transformed into healing powers at another season. If we know what is going on mysteriously in the products and beings of nature, we learn to recognize their therapeutic power. It is the same with the luciferic element: we learn to recognize the healing forces active in volatile substances that rise up from the earth, and especially those present in carbon dioxide. For just as I explained that in all water there is a mercurial, quicksilver element, so in carbon dioxide there is always a sulphurous, phosphoric element.

There is no carbon dioxide which consists simply—as the chemists say—of one carbon atom and two oxygen atoms; no such thing exists. In the carbon dioxide we breathe out there is always a phosphoric, sulphurous element. This carbon dioxide, CO_2, one atom of carbon and two of oxygen, is merely an abstraction, an intellectual concept formed in the human mind. In reality there is no carbon dioxide which does not contain a phosphoric, sulphurous element in an extremely diluted state, and the luciferic beings strive towards it in the rising vapour.

Again, we see in this peculiar balance between the sulphur element that becomes astral and the limestone that becomes living the expression of the forces we can recognize as healing influences.

And so, among many other things connected with the Easter mystery, this mystery play at Easter, especially because of its enactment in front of the painting and the sculpture, would round off, for those who had the will to hear it, all that had been brought in the course of the year concerning various kinds of therapy, and this in a manner that could be artistically religious in a directly living way. This would indeed find its rightful place by being set into the cosmos and the seasons; and then the Easter festival would embrace something that could be expressed in the words: 'The presence of the World Healer is felt—the Saviour who willed to lift the great evil from the world. His presence is felt.' For in truth He was, as I have often said, the great Physician in the evolution of mankind. This will be felt, and to Him will sacrifice be offered in the form of all the wisdom about healing influences that man can possess. This would be included in the Easter mystery, the Easter ritual; and by celebrating the Easter festival in this way we should be placing it quite naturally in the context of the seasonal course of the year.

To begin with, in describing the powerful Imaginations that come before man at Michaelmas and Christmas, I was able to show them to you only as pictures. But in the case of the Easter Imagination, where over against the activities of the nature spirits arises the higher life of the spirit, as this can develop in the vicinity of the Christ, I could show how Imagination can lead directly to a ritual in the earthly realm, a ritual embracing things which must be cherished and preserved on earth—the health-giving healing forces, and a knowledge of the ahrimanic and luciferic forces which could destroy the human organism. For Ahriman hardens human beings, while Lucifer wishes to dissolve and evaporate them through their breathing. In all this the forces that make for illness reside.

All that can be learnt in this way under the influence of the great teacher Raphael—who is really Mercury in Christian terminology, and in Christian usage should carry the staff of Mercury—can find its worthy consummation only in so far as it is received into the mysteries and ritual of Easter, which include a great deal more than this, and this I shall bring another time.

Lecture 4

THE ST JOHN IMAGINATION

If we now go forward from Easter, the spring festival, we shall need to penetrate much more spiritually into the subject than we had to do in considering the previous seasons of the year. This may sound like a contradiction, but it is not so. In thinking of the Christmas season we had to start from the way in which earthly material limestone is gradually transformed, and we carried this thought over to the time of Easter. In general, we have been observing the active working of the spiritual in the material realm. Now at midsummer humanity is really enmeshed within the being of nature. From spring onwards into summer, the nature process becomes constantly more active, more inwardly saturated, and human beings become thoroughly inter-woven in this nature process. We can indeed say that in high summer human beings experience a kind of nature-consciousness. During spring, if they have the perception and feeling for it, they become one with all that is growing and sprouting. They blossom with the flower, germinate with the plant, fruit with the plant, enter into everything that lives and has its being in the world outside. In this way they project their personality into the being of nature, and a kind of nature-consciousness arises in them. Then, since in autumn nature dies away and thus bears death within itself, human beings too, if they participate in what autumn—the time of Michaelmas—means for nature, must also experi-ence this death within themselves. But in their own selves they must not take part in it; they must raise themselves above it. Precisely when nature-consciousness is strongest a strengthening of their self-consciousness must occur. But in the glow of summer, just because a nature-consciousness is then at its height in humanity, it is all the more necessary for the cosmos that—if only human beings are willing—the cosmos should bring the spiritual to meet them.

Hence we can say: In summer human beings are closely enmeshed in nature but, if they have the right feeling and perception for it, objective spirituality comes towards them from nature's interweaving life. And so, to find the essential human being during St John's time, at midsummer we must turn to the objective spirituality in the outer world, and this is present everywhere in nature. Only in outward appearance is nature the sprouting, budding—one might say the sleeping—being which calls forth from the powers of sleep the forces of vegetative growth, in which a kind of sleeping nature-life is given form. But in this sleeping nature, if only human beings have the perception for it, the spirit that animates and weaves through everything in nature is revealed.

So it is that if at midsummer we follow nature with deepened spiritual insight and with perceptive eyes, we find our gaze directed to the depths of the earth itself. We find that the minerals down there display their inner crystal-forming process more vividly than at any other time of the year. If we look with imaginative perception into the depths of the earth at St John's-tide, we really have the impression that down there are the crystalline forms into which the hard earth consolidates—the very crystalline forms that gain their full beauty at the height of summer. At midsummer everything down below the earth shapes itself into lines, angles and surfaces. If we are to have an impression of it as a whole, we must picture this crystallizing process as an interweaving activity, coloured throughout with deep blue.

I will try to show it on the blackboard, though of course I can do so only in a quite sketchy way [Plate 5]. So we can say: On looking downwards we have an impression of linear forms, suffused with blue, and everywhere the blue is shot through with lines that sparkle like silver, so that everywhere within the silver-sparkling blue the crystallizing process [white] can be discerned. It is as though nature wishes to present her formative power in a wonderfully mobile design, but a design that cannot be seen in the way we see with our ordinary sight. It is seen in such a way that one really feels oneself dissolved into the mobile design, and feels every silver-gleaming line down there to be within oneself, part of oneself. One feels that as a human form one has grown out of the blue depths of the earth's crust, and one feels inwardly permeated with force by the silver-gleaming crystal lines. All this seems part of one's own being. And if one comes to oneself and asks, 'How is it that these silver-sparkling crystal lines and waves are working within myself? What is it that lives and works there, silver-gleaming in the blue of the earth?' Then one knows: That is cosmic Will.

And when gazing downwards one has the feeling of rising out of cosmic Will.

This is how it is when one looks down into the depths of the earth. And what does one see if one looks up to the heights? The impression is of out-spreading cosmic Intelligence. Human intelligence — as I have often said — is not worth much at its present stage. But the heavens at midsummer give one the feeling that cosmic Intelligence is active everywhere — the intelligence not of single beings but of many beings who live together and within one another. Thus we have up there the out-spreading Intelligence woven through with light; living Intelligence shining forth [yellow] as the polar opposite of Will. And while we feel that down below — in that blue darkness everything is experienced only as forces, up above we feel — everything is such that in perceiving it we are illumined, permeated, with a feeling of intelligence.

And now within this radiant activity there appears — I

cannot put it otherwise — a Form. When we were speaking of autumn, I had to name Michael as the significant figure who rises before our souls out of the weaving of nature. As to how Gabriel — to use the old name — enters into the time of Christmas, we shall have more to say. In the last lecture I showed you how at Easter, the season of spring, the figure of Raphael comes before us. He comes in dramatic guise, as the mediator who arouses in us the proper approach, through reverence and worship, to what the Easter Imagination, the cosmic Easter Imagination, is. And now, for St John's-time, there appears — to describe it in human terms, which are of course bound to be only approximate — an extraordinary earnest countenance. It arises glowing warmly out of the pervading radiant Intelligence [red head in the yellow, Plate 5]. We have the impression that this figure forms its warm body of light out of the radiant Intelligence. And for this to happen at the height of summer something I have already described must arise: the elemental spirits of the earth must soar upwards. As they do so, they weave themselves into the shining Intelligence up above, and the shining Intelligence receives them into itself. And out of that gleaming radiance the figure I have just mentioned takes form.

This form was divined by the old instinctive clairvoyance, and we can give it the same name by which it was known then. We can say: In summer, Uriel appears in the midst of the shining Intelligence.

Autumn	Michael
Winter	Gabriel
Spring	Raphael
Summer	Uriel

It is with great earnestness that this representative of the weaving cosmic forces appears in the time of summer, seeking to embody himself in a vesture of light. There are more things we can observe as the deeds accomplished by

Uriel in the radiant light — Uriel, whose own Intelligence arises fundamentally from the working together of the planetary forces of our planetary system, supported by the working of the fixed stars of the zodiac; Uriel, who in his thought cherishes the thoughts of the cosmos. And so, quite directly, the feeling comes: You clouds of summer, radiant with Intelligence, in which the blue crystal formations of the earth below are reflected upwards, just as these blue crystal formations mirror in turn the shining Intelligence of the summer clouds — out of your shining in high summer an earnest countenance appears, a concentrated Imagination of cosmic Understanding.

Now the deeds of this embodied cosmic Understanding, this cosmic Intelligence, are woven in light. Through the power of attraction in the concentrated cosmic Intelligence of Uriel, the silver forces [white] are drawn upwards, and in the light of this inwardly shining Intelligence, as seen from the earth, they appear as radiant sunlight, densifying into a glory of gold. One has the immediate feeling that the gleaming silver, streaming up from below, is received by the sunlit radiance above. And the earth-silver — the phrase is quite correct — is changed by cosmic alchemy into the cosmic gold living and weaving in the heights.

If we follow these happenings further, during August, we gain an impression of something that complements the form of Michael, already described. I told you what the sword of Michael is made of, and whence the dragon draws his coiling life. But now, in the radiant beauty that appears spiritually out of the cosmic weaving at the height of summer, we ask ourselves: Whence does Michael, who leads us over to autumn, to the time of Michaelmas, derive his characteristic raiment — the raiment which first lights up in golden sunshine and then inwardly as a silver-sparkling radiance within the golden folds? Where does Michael acquire this gold-woven, silver-sparkling raiment? It comes from what is formed in the heights through the upward-raying silver and the gold that flows to meet it; from the transmutation by the sun's power of the silver sparkling upwards from the earth. As autumn approaches we see how the silver given by the earth to the cosmos returns as gold, and the power of this transmuted silver is the source of what happens in the earth during winter, as I have described. The sun-gold, formed in the heights, in the dominion of Uriel during high summer, passes down to weave and flow through the depths of the earth, where it animates the elements that in the midst of winter are seeking to become the living growth of the following year.

So you see that when we come to the time of sprouting, springing life we can no longer speak of matter permeated by spirit, as we speak of the earth in winter. We have to speak of spirit woven through with matter — that is, with silver and gold. Of course you must not take all this too literally; you must think of the silver and gold as diluted far beyond the level of human comprehension. Then you will come to feel that all this is a kind of background for the cosmic, light-filled deeds of Uriel, and a clear impression of the countenance and gaze of Uriel will appear before you.

We feel a deep longing to understand this remarkable gaze, directed downwards, and we have the impression we must look around to find out what it signifies. Its meaning first dawns upon the mind when as human beings we learn to penetrate with spiritual vision still more deeply into the blue, silver-gleaming depths of the earth in summer. And we see that weaving around these silver-gleaming crystalline rays are shapes — disturbing shapes, I might almost call them — which continually gather and dissolve, gather and dissolve.

Then we come to perceive — the vision will be different for everyone — that these shapes are human errors which stand out in contrast to the natural order of regular crystals here below. And it is on this contrast that Uriel directs his earnest gaze. Here during the height of summer the imperfections of mankind, in contrast to the regularity of the growing crystal forms, are searchingly scanned. Here it is that from the earnest gaze of Uriel we gain the impression of how the moral is interwoven with the natural world order. Here the moral world order does not exist only in ourselves as abstract impulses. For whereas we habitually look at the realms of nature without asking whether there is morality in the growth of plants, or in the process of crystallization—now we see how at midsummer human errors are woven into the regular crystals which are formed in the normal course of nature.

On the other hand, everything of the nature of human virtue and human excellence rises up with the silver-gleaming lines and is seen as the clouds that envelop Uriel [red]. It enters into the radiant Intelligence, transmuted into cloud-shaped works of art.

It is impossible to behold the increasingly earnest gaze of Uriel, directed towards the depths of the earth, without also seeing there something like winglike arms, or armlike wings, raised in earnest admonition, and this gesture of Uriel's rouses in mankind what I might call the historic conscience. Here at midsummer there appears this historic conscience, which at the present time has become uncommonly feeble. It appears, as it were, in Uriel's warning gesture.

You must picture all this of course as an Imagination. These things are quite real, but I cannot speak of them in the way a physicist speaks of positive and negative, of potential energy and so on. I have to speak in pictures that will come to life in your souls. But everything expressed in these living pictures is reality; it is there.

And now if we have come to perceive the connection existing between human morality and the crystalline element below and between human virtues and the shining beauty above, and if we take these connections into our inner experience, the real St John Imagination will appear to us. For the St John Imagination is there, just as we have the Michael Imagination, the Christmas Imagination and the Easter Imagination.

So to spiritual observation this picture appears as a kind of culmination. Above, illuminated as it were by the power of Uriel's eyes, the Dove [white]. The silver-sparkling blue below, arising from the depths of the earth and bound up with human weaknesses and error, is gathered into a picture of the Earth Mother [blue]. Whether she is called Demeter or Mary, the picture is of the Earth Mother. So it is that in directing our gaze downwards we cannot do otherwise than bring together in Imagination all those secrets of the depths which go to make up the Earth Mother of all existence; while in all that is concentrated in the flowing form above we feel and experience the Spirit Father of everything around us. And now we behold the outcome of the working together of Spirit Father with Earth Mother, bearing so beautifully within itself the harmony of the earthly silver and the gold of the heights. Between the Father and the Mother we behold the Son [Plate 5]. Thus there arises this Imagination of the Trinity which is really the St John Imagination. The background of it is Uriel, the creative, admonishing Uriel.

What the Trinity truly represents should not be placed dogmatically before the soul, for then an impression is given that such an idea, or picture, of the Trinity can be separated from the weaving of cosmic life. This is not so. At midsummer the Trinity reveals itself out of the midst of cosmic life, cosmic activity. It comes forth with inwardly convincing power, if — I might say — one has first penetrated into the mysteries of Uriel. If we were to present St John's-tide in this way, there would have to be an arched or vaulted background, with the figure of Uriel and his gesture in the manner I have described. And against this background a living picture of the imagination of the Trinity would have to arise. Special arrangements would be necessary; the effect would have to be that of painting done instantaneously, perhaps by making artistic use of vaporous substances or the like. And if we conjure up the true Imagination of these things for people to witness, it must be at St John's-time. At Easter we have the complete picture only when we bring it into dramatic form, with Raphael present as a teacher in the mystery play that would have then to be presented; Raphael who leads mankind into the secrets of healing nature, of the healing cosmos. In a similar way, at St John's-time, all that can then be seen in weaving pictures would have to be transposed into powerful music, so that the cosmic mystery, as it can be experienced by mankind at this season of St John, would speak to our hearts.

We must imagine how all that I have described should find artistic expression, on the one hand, in the fine arts. But what is experienced in this way must be given life by the musical tones embodying the poetic motif which plays through our souls when we feel our way to great Uriel, active in the light, who calls up in us a powerful impression of the Trinity. The silver gleam that rays up from below, and is revealed in the form-giving beauty of the light above, must be expressed at St John's-tide through appropriate musical instrumentation. Thus we should find, through these musical harmonies, our own inner harmony with the cosmos, for in them the secret of our coexistence with the cosmos at St John's-tide would have to sound forth. All this would have to be given voice in the music, so that in looking up to the heights we would be looking at the weaving gold of the cosmos, and would see the glowing form of Uriel emerging from the light-filled gold and directing his gaze and his gesture down to the earth, as I have described. All this would have to be not in any fixed form but in living movement. That would be one motif, a heavenly motif through which we can feel ourselves united, on one side, with the shining cosmic Intelligence.

On the other hand in the depths we feel ourselves united with the tendency to fixed form, with what is immersed in the bluish darkness from out of which the silvery radiance streams forth. Down there we feel the material foundation of active spiritual being. The heights become mysteries, the depths become mysteries, and human beings themselves become a mystery within the mysteries of the cosmos. Right into their bony system human beings feel the crystal-forming power. But they feel also how this same power is in cosmic union with the living power of light in the heavens above. They feel how all the morality taking place in humanity lives and has its being both in these mysteries of the heights and in these mysteries of the depths, and in the uniting of them both. They feel that they are no longer sundered from the world around them but placed within it, united above with the shining Intelligence in which they experience, as in the womb of worlds, their own best thoughts. They feel themselves united below, right into their bony system, with the cosmic crystallizing force — and they feel the two united with one another again. They feel their death united with the spirit-life of the universe; and they feel how this spirit-life craves to awaken and create the crystal forces and the silver-gleaming life in the midst of earthly death.

All this, too, would have to resound in musical tones — tones which carry these motifs on their wings and make them part of human experience. For these motifs are there. They do not have to be invented; they can be read from the cosmic activity of Uriel. Here it is that Imagination passes over into Inspiration.

Man, however, lives in a certain sense as an embodied Inspiration, as a being brought into existence by Inspiration, in the mysteries of the heights and depths and in the mysteries of their conjunction. He lives in the mysteries to which the Spirit Father points upward, the mysteries to which the Earth Mother points downward, the mysteries which are united by the fact that the Christ, through the working together of the Spirit Father and the Earth Mother, stands directly before the human soul as the sustaining Cosmic Spirit.

What is woven out of all these cosmic secrets I may put before you somewhat as follows. It is as though the human being, placed in the midst of all that goes on at midsummer, were to feel something like this. The first words endeavour to represent how the gaze of Uriel concentrates itself into Inspiration, united with the Spirit tones of the whole choir:

Schaue unser Weben
Das leuchtende Erregen } The heights
Das wärmende Leben

Lebe irdisch Erhaltendes
Und atmend Gestaltetes } The depths
Als wesenhaft Waltendes

Fühle dein Menschengebeine } The centre
Mit himmlischem Scheine } The inner being
Im waltenden Weltenvereine } of man

Behold the active flow
the germinating glow
Of our warmth-engendering life

Experience and live
The all-pervading being
Maintaining things of earth
And things formed of the breath

Feel how your very bones
Share in the heavenly glory
Through the power and strength
Of the union of worlds

Here in these nine lines [in the German] are the mysteries of the heights, the mysteries of the depths, the mysteries of the centre, which are also those of the inner being of man. And then we have the whole gathered up as a cosmic statement of these mysteries of the heights, the depths and the centre, sounding as though with organ and trumpet tones:

Es werden Stoffe verdichtet
Es werden Fehler gerichtet
Es werden Herzen gesichtet.

[Substances are densified, errors are judged and rectified, hearts are sifted.]

Here you have that which can permeate the human being at midsummer, supporting him, exalting him, strengthening him — the St John Imagination filled with Inspiration, the St John Inspiration filled with Imagination — in these words:

Schaue unser Weben
Das leuchtende Erregen   } The heights
Das wärmende Leben

Lebe irdisch Erhaltendes
Und atmend Gestaltetes   } The depths
Als wesenhaft Waltendes

Fühle dein Menschengebeine   The centre
Mit himmlischen Scheine   } The inner being
Im waltenden Weltenvereine   of man

Es werden Stoffe verdichtet
Es werden Fehler gerichtet
Es werden Herzen gesichtet.

Lecture 5

THE WORKING TOGETHER OF THE FOUR ARCHANGELS

During the last few days I have brought before you the four cosmic Imaginations that can be invoked through an intimate human experience of the seasons of the year. If we want to arrive at an understanding of mankind's circumstances and situation in the world, we must seek it in the interworking of those beings who appear in conjunction with these imaginative pictures. And here I would like first to say something by way of introduction.

If we open our souls to the impressions that may come to us from the content of these pictures, then at the same time there will come to us much that has been experienced in the course of human evolution as an echo of old, instinctive clairvoyance. Today this is sometimes merely quoted as history, but fundamentally it is not understood. True poets and spiritually inspired people give ear to these often wonderful voices resounding from the traditions of the past, and use them just when they wish to express their highest and greatest conceptions. But even then they are very little understood. Thus in the first part of *Faust* a wonderful utterance rings out which is hardly at all understood, though it is quoted often enough. It occurs when Faust, having opened the book of Nostradamus, comes upon the sign of the macrocosm:

> *Wie alles sich zum Ganzen webt,*
> *Eins in dem andern wirkt und lebt!*
> *Wie Himmelskräfte auf- und niedersteigen*
> *Und sich die goldnen Eimer reichen,*

Mit segenduftenden Schwingen
Von Himmel durch die Erde dringen,
Harmonisch all das All durchklingen!

How each the Whole its substance gives,
each in the other works and lives!
See heavenly forces rising and descending,
their golden urns reciprocally lending:
on wings that winnow sweet blessing
from heaven through the earth they're pressing,
to fill the All with harmonies caressing.*

A magnificent picture—but if one knows Goethe one must say that it is real to him only through his *feelings*. For what Goethe has evidently drawn from his reading of old traditions and his feeling for them—all this stands in its full significance before our souls only if we have in mind the four great cosmic Imaginations, as I described them to you—the autumn Imagination of Michael, the Christmas Imagination of Gabriel, the Easter Imagination of Raphael, and the Midsummer, St John's Day, Imagination of Uriel. You must really picture to yourselves how from all these beings, Gabriel, Raphael, Uriel, Michael, forces stream out through the cosmos and as formative forces stream again into mankind. In order to understand this, we must see how a human being stands within the cosmos in—I might almost call it—a purely material way.

In this connection there is very little understanding, unfortunately, for how things really are. For example, medical textbooks always describe how human beings breathe in oxygen from the air and how the carbon within them takes up the oxygen; this process is then compared with external combustion, in which all sorts of external substances combine with oxygen. The whole process in the

---

*From the translation of *Faust*, Part One, by Bayard Taylor, revised and edited by Stuart Atkins. Published by Collier Books, New York, 1962.

human organism, whereby oxygen is taken up by carbon, is then called combustion.

All this is said because one essential fact is not known — the fact that all external substances and processes become different directly they enter into the human organism. Anyone who speaks of this peculiar combination of oxygen and carbon in human beings and thinks of it as combustion is talking in just the same way as if someone said: 'There is no need for a person to have two living lungs; he could equally well have a pair of stones suspended inside him.' That is more or less how people talk in speaking of the combustion of oxygen and carbon within the human organism.

Everything that takes place externally in nature becomes different as soon as it enters human beings. No process within the human organism takes place in the same way as in outer nature. A flame that burns externally is dead fire; what corresponds within the human being is living and ensouled flame.

You might as well compare a stone with a lung as an external flame with the living activity in the human organism when carbon unites with oxygen there — a process which, viewed externally, is indeed combustion in chemical terms. Today all spiritual progress depends on our being able to grasp these things in the right way. Suppose you take salt with your food, or eat some protein or whatever; people assume that it remains just the same substance within you as it was outside. That is not true. Whatever enters the human being changes immediately. And the forces which make it different proceed in a quite definite way from those beings whom I have pictured in the four Imaginations.

Let us now recall the last picture: how at St John's-tide Uriel hovers in the heights, weaving his body out of golden light in the golden radiance of the sun [Plate 5, red]. As I told you, we must picture him with grave, discriminating eyes, for his gaze is directed down towards the crystal realm of the earth, and he sees how little compatible human errors are with the abstract but none the less shining beauty of the crystallization process that goes on below the surface of the earth. That is the reason for his gravely judging gaze, as he looks down and compares human errors with the living activity in the crystals of the earth.

I spoke also of Uriel's gesture as a warning gesture, indicating to human beings what they *ought* to do. It calls upon them, if they understand it aright, to transform their faults into virtues. For up above in the clouds there appear the shining pictures of beauty, woven out of the sun-gold, and they are pictures of all that humanity has achieved by way of virtue.

Now from the being who has to be described in this way—and can be described in no other way—proceed forces that work directly in mankind and continue to work further in a characteristic way. All that I am depicting takes place at midsummer. The Uriel being is not at rest but in majestic movement. This must be so, for when it is summer with us it is winter in the opposite hemisphere, and Uriel is there in the heights. We must picture this clearly, so that if we have the earth here [see sketch] Uriel appears to us in summer, and then in the course of six months he has reached the other side. Then it is winter with us.

While Uriel descends [yellow arrow] and while his forces are thus coming to us from a descending line, summer with us passes over into winter, and then Uriel is over the other hemisphere. But the earth does not hinder his forces from coming to us; they penetrate through the earth. Hence we can say that the forces which come to us directly from above [red arrows], seeking to permeate us with the sun-gold of summer, penetrate right through the earth in winter and permeate us in an ascending stream [red] from the other side.

If we bring before our souls how at midsummer Uriel

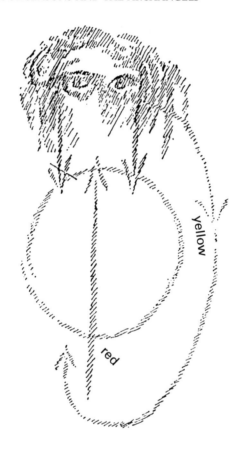

works through nature into humanity—for his activity streams into the forces of nature—we must picture the forces of Uriel streaming out into the cosmos, raying into the clouds, the rain, the thunder and lightning, and raying also into the growth of plants. In winter, after Uriel has made his way round the earth, his forces stream up through the earth and come to rest in our heads. And then these forces, which at other times are outside in nature, work through us to make us citizens of the cosmos. For they actually cause an image of the cosmos to arise in our heads, illuminating us so that we acquire human wisdom.

We speak correctly if we say: Uriel makes his descent as summer passes through autumn into winter. Then in winter he begins to reascend, and from this descending and ascending power of Uriel we get the inner forces of our heads. Thus Uriel works in nature at midsummer and during the winter season he works in the human head, so that in this connection human beings are truly a microcosm in relation to the macrocosm.

We understand the human being only if we picture him not merely as a being of nature but as a spiritual being. And just as we can follow the forces of Uriel and see how they stream into mankind through the course of the year, we must also do this with Raphael, who pours his forces into the forces of nature in spring, as I have described. I had to show you how the Easter Imagination is supplemented by the teaching that Raphael, the great cosmic physician, can give to mankind. For precisely when we allow all that Raphael brings about, working in the springtime forces of nature as Uriel does in summer, when we allow all this to work on us at Easter through the spiritual healing of Inspiration, then we have the crowning of all the truths of healing for mankind.

But the springtime activity of Raphael travels round the earth, in a similar way to Uriel's. In terms of the cosmos Uriel is the spirit of summer; he moves round the earth and in winter creates the inner forces of the human head. Raphael is the spirit of spring, and in autumn, as he travels round the earth, he engenders the forces of human breathing. Hence we can say: While during autumn Michael is the cosmic spirit up above, the cosmic Archangel, at Michaelmas Raphael works in human beings — Raphael who is active in the whole human breathing system, regulating it and giving it his blessing. And we shall form a true picture of autumn only if on the one hand we have, up above, the powerful Michael Imagination, with the sword forged from meteoric iron, the garment woven out of sun-gold and shot through with the earth's silver-sparkling radiance, while down below Raphael is working in mankind, aware of every breath that is drawn, of everything that flows from the lungs into the heart and from the heart through the whole circulation of the blood. Thus human beings learn to recognize in themselves the healing forces that play through the cosmos in the Raphael time of spring, if in autumn, when the rays of Raphael pass through the earth, they come to know how Raphael is active in human breathing.

For this is a great secret: all the healing forces reside originally in the human breathing system. And anyone who truly understands the whole dimension of the breath knows the healing forces from the human side. They do not reside in the other systems of the human organism; these other systems have themselves to be healed.

Look up what I have said about it with regard to education: the breathing system is especially active between the ages of seven and fourteen. There are great possibilities of illness during the first seven years of life, and again after fourteen; they are relatively least during the period when the breath pulses through the body with the help of the etheric body. A secret activity of healing resides in the breathing system, and all the secrets of healing are at the same time secrets of breathing. And this is connected with the fact that the workings of Raphael, which are cosmic in spring, permeate, in autumn, the whole mystery of human breathing.

We have learnt to know Gabriel as the Christmas Archangel. He is then the Cosmic Spirit; we have to look up above to find him. During the summer Gabriel carries into mankind all that is brought about by the formative forces of nourishment. At midsummer they are brought into mankind by the Gabriel forces, after Gabriel has descended from his cosmic activity during the winter to his human activity in the summer, when his forces stream through the earth and it is winter on the other side.

And when at last we come to Michael, he is our Cosmic Spirit in autumn. He is then at his highest; he has reached his cosmic culmination. Then he begins his descent; in spring his forces penetrate up through the earth and live in all that comes to expression in human beings as movement and the power of will, enabling them to walk and work and take hold of things.

Now place the full pictures before you. First, the summer picture at the time of St John: up above the grave countenance of Uriel, with his judgmental look, his warning mien and gesture; and, drawing near to human beings and permeating them, the mild and loving gaze of Gabriel, Gabriel with his gesture of blessing. So during summer we have the working together of Uriel in the cosmos, Gabriel on the human side.

If we pass on to autumn, we have not the commanding but rather the guiding look of Michael. For seen in the right light, Michael's gaze is like a pointer, as though wishing not to look inwards but outwards into the world. His gaze is positive, active. And his sword forged out of cosmic iron is held so that at the same time he indicates to human beings their way. That is the picture up above.

Below, in autumn, is Raphael, with deeply thoughtful gaze, bringing to mankind the healing forces that he has first, one might say, kindled in the cosmos — Raphael, with deep wisdom in his gaze, leaning on the staff of Mercury, supported by the inner forces of the earth. Thus we have the working together of Michael in the cosmos, Raphael on earth.

Now we go on to winter. Gabriel is then the cosmic Angel; Gabriel is up above, with his mild and loving look and his gesture of benediction, weaving his garment of snow in the clouds of winter. And below is Uriel, with his grave judgment and warning, at the side of humanity. The positions are reversed.

And as we come round again to spring, up above we find

Raphael with his deeply thoughtful gaze, with his staff of Mercury (which now in the airy heights has become something like a fiery serpent, a serpent of shining fire), no longer leaning it on the earth but as though holding it in front of him, using the forces of the air, mingling and combining fire, water and earth so as to transmute them into healing forces working and weaving in the cosmos.

And below, becoming especially visible, is Michael, coming to meet mankind with his positive gaze, showing the way into the world and glad to draw our eyes in the same direction, as he stands close to mankind, the complement of Raphael, in spring.

So now we have the pictures:

Winter: Gabriel above, Uriel below
Spring: Raphael above, Michael below
Summer: Uriel above, Gabriel below, with mankind
Autumn: Michael above, Raphael below, with mankind

Now let us take the words which have come down through the ages like an old magical utterance and were used again by Goethe:

How each the Whole its substance gives,
each in the other works and lives!

Yes, indeed, Uriel, Gabriel, Raphael and Michael work together, one working in the other, living in the other, and when the human being is placed in the universe as a being of spirit, soul and body, these forces work magically in him. And how far-reaching is the truth in these words, how far they go! Think what they mean:

How each the Whole its substance gives,
each in the other works and lives!
See heavenly forces rising and descending,

—rising and descending! And then the lines that follow:

their golden urns reciprocally lending:
on wings that winnow sweet blessing
from heaven through the earth they're pressing,
to fill the All with harmonies caressing.

Remember how in yesterday's lecture I spoke of it all passing over from sculptural form into musical sound, universally resounding harmony.

I cannot tell you what I felt when this came before my soul and I read again these lines by Goethe: *From heaven through the earth they're pressing!* This *through* — it can shake one profoundly, for that is just how it is — it is true! It is staggering to realize that these words ring through the world like a peal of bells and are regarded as poetic licence or something of the sort — or as words that anyone might write in letters or articles. It is not so. These are words which correspond to a cosmic fact. It is really shattering to read these words in the context of Goethe's *Faust* and to know how true they are.

Now we will go further. We have seen how the heavenly Powers with golden pinions — the Archangels — permeate the universe in harmony, working and living in one another. But that is not all.

Let us look at Gabriel, who draws nutritive forces out of the cosmos and brings them into humanity at midsummer. These forces are active in the human metabolic system.

Raphael controls the breathing system. And now Gabriel and Raphael, as they ascend and descend, work together in such a way that Gabriel passes up into the breathing system those forces of his which are otherwise active in human nutrition, and there they become healing forces. Gabriel hands on the nourishment to Raphael, and it then becomes a means of healing. When what is otherwise only a nutritive process in the human organism is interwoven with the secret of breathing, it becomes a healing force.

We must indeed observe carefully the transformation

that external substances undergo in the nutritive system itself; then we come to recognize the significance of the Gabriel forces, the nutritive forces, in mankind. But these forces are led over into the breathing system. And in working on further there, they become not only a means of quenching hunger and thirst, not only restorative forces: they turn into forces for the inner correction of illness. The transmuted nutritive forces become healing forces. Anyone who understands nutrition correctly understands the first stage of healing. If he knows what salt should do in a healthy person, then, if he allows the metamorphosis from the Gabriel way of working to the Raphael way to work on him, he will know how salt can act as a means of healing in one or another case. The healing forces within us are metamorphoses of the nutritive forces. Raphael receives the golden vessel of nutrition from Gabriel; it is passed on to him.

And now we come to a secret, familiar in ancient times but entirely lost today. Anyone who can read Hippocrates,

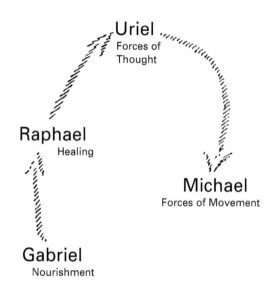

Uriel
Forces of
Thought

Raphael
Healing

Michael
Forces of Movement

Gabriel
Nourishment

or even if he cannot read Galen can still gather something from him, will notice that in Hippocrates, and even in Galen — those old physicians — something still survived which is really a great human secret. The forces that prevail in our breathing system are healing forces; they are healing us continually. But when these breathing forces rise into our heads, the healing forces become spiritual forces, active in sense perception and in thinking. Here is the secret that was known at one time — the secret that is almost explicit in Hippocrates and can at least be deduced from Galen. Thought, perception, the inner spiritual life of humanity, are a higher metamorphosis of therapy, of the healing process; and when the healing element in the breathing system, which lies between the head and the digestive system, is driven further up, as it were, it becomes the material foundation for the spiritual life of humanity.

So we can say: The thoughts which flash through the human head are really a transmutation of the healing impulses that reside in the various substances. Hence if a person really understands this then he can look at a healing salt substance or some remedial plant substance and say: In this context you are a beneficial healing force, which I can give to someone if he needs it. But if this substance enters a person and passes beyond the realm of breathing so that it works in his head it becomes the material bearer of the power of thought, for Raphael then hands on his vessel to Uriel. What Raphael has received from the realm of nourishment and transmuted into healing forces he hands over to Uriel, and it then becomes the power of thinking.

Why does a remedy heal? Because it is on the way to the spirit. And if one knows how far on the way to the spirit a remedy is, one knows its healing power. The spirit cannot of itself lay hold directly on the earthly element in mankind, but the lower stage of the spirit is a therapeutic force.

And just as Gabriel passes on to Raphael the nutritive forces, to be transmuted into forces of healing — in other words, passes on his golden vessel—and just as Raphael passes on his golden vessel to Uriel, whereby the healing forces are made into the forces of thought, so it is Michael who receives from Uriel the thought forces, and through the power of cosmic iron, out of which his sword is forged, transforms these thought forces into forces of will, so that in mankind they become the forces of movement.

Hence we have this second picture: Uriel, Raphael, Gabriel and Michael, ascending and descending; Uriel and Gabriel, let us say, working in one another, but also working with one another, one giving what he possesses to the other, so that it can work on further in him. We see how the heavenly Powers rise and descend, passing to one another golden vessels—the golden vessels of nourishment, of healing, of the forces of thinking and of movement. Thus these golden vessels move on from one Archangel to another, while at the same time each Archangel works with the other in cosmic harmony.

And again in *Faust* we find:

See heavenly forces rising and descending,
their golden urns reciprocally lending!

True indeed, down to the very word 'golden', for these things are woven out of the sun-gold radiating from Uriel, as I described yesterday.

Goethe had of course read the words to which he then gave poetic expression, and it made a tremendous impression on him. But the interpretation I have been able to picture for you here—that he did not know. It is just this which staggers one—to find that when out of a certain poetic feeling a spirit such as Goethe's takes hold of something handed down from old traditions it so incredibly reflects the truth! This is the splendid thing that unites us, that in cultivating spiritual science today these things are revealed to us: when we see for ourselves how Uriel and Raphael and Michael and Gabriel are working together, and how they really do pass on to one another their own particular forces. If we first see this for ourselves and then, having perhaps indirectly come across an ancient picture, in this case through Goethe, we let it work upon us, we see how an old instinctive truth—no matter whether mythical or legendary— was at one time widely current in the world. And then times change, and in our own time we see how the ancient truth has to be raised to a higher level.

O Hippocrates—it is all the same whether we now give the name of Raphael, Mercury or Hermes to the one who stood at his side—this Hippocrates lived at a time when twilight was falling over the knowledge of this joint working of Gabriel, Raphael and Uriel, and of the way the healing forces in the human organism lie between the thoughts and the nutritive forces. This was the source from which an ancient instinctive wisdom drew those wonderful old remedies which in fact have again and again been renewed. Today they are found among so-called primitive peoples, and nobody can imagine how they have been come by. All this is connected with the fact that mankind once possessed a primeval wisdom.

But now there must really be a problem left in your minds. It is this. If you take everything I have put before you—how, for example, the Raphael forces are active in spring, and in autumn they are carried over by Raphael into the inwardness of the breathing system—you must have been led to suppose that humanity is entirely caught up in the working of the forces of the cosmos throughout the course of the year. Originally, indeed, that is how it was. But because a human being is the kind of being who remembers what happens to him, so that an outer experience is preserved in memory and after days or years can be relived as an inner experience, so these truths, which are entirely valid for the cosmos, continue to run their course. However, a human being does not experience the Raphael force inwardly in his breathing system only in the autumn, but on through the winter, summer and spring. A kind of memory of it, more substantial than ordinary memory, remains.

So while things are arranged in the way I have described, their effects work on in human beings throughout the year. As an experience remains fixed in the memory, so these effects continue all through the year; otherwise human beings could not be uniformly developing beings all the year round. In physical life one person forgets more readily or less readily than another. But the influence Raphael has planted in our breathing system during the autumn would disappear by the following autumn if Raphael did not come again. Until then this nature-memory in the breathing organ remains active, but then it has to be renewed.

So human beings are nevertheless placed into the cycle of the year; they are not excluded from the world's course but planted in the midst of it. But they are placed there in yet another way. It is true that a human being, standing here on earth, enclosed within his skin, with his organs embedded in his body, feels himself somewhat isolated in the cosmos, for the connections I have described are indeed full of mystery. But this is not the case when a human being is in a soul-spiritual form, for example during his pre-earthly existence. Between death and a new birth he lives in a realm of spirit. His soul gazes down not at an individual human body—it chooses this in the course of time—but at the whole earth, and indeed at the earth in connection with the whole planetary system, and with all the interwoven activities of Raphael, Uriel, Gabriel and Michael. In that realm one is looking at oneself from outside.

It is there that the door opens for the entry of souls who are returning from pre-earthly life. It opens only during the period from the end of December to the beginning of spring, when Gabriel hovers above as cosmic Archangel, while below at mankind's side is Uriel, carrying cosmic forces into the human head. In the course of these three months the souls who are to be embodied during the whole of the coming year come down from the cosmos towards the earth. They remain waiting there until an opportunity occurs in the earth's planetary sphere. Even the souls who will be born in October, let us say, are already within the earth-sphere, awaiting their birth. Basically, a great deal depends on whether a soul, after it has entered the earth-sphere and is already in touch with it, still has to wait for its earthly embodiment. One soul has a longer wait, another a shorter one.

The particular secret here is that — just as, for example, the fructifying seed enters the ovum at only one spot — the heavenly seeds enter into the whole yearly being of the earth only when Gabriel rules above as the cosmic Angel, with his mild, loving look and gesture of benediction, while below there is Uriel, with his judgmental gaze and warning gesture. That is the time when the earth is impregnated with souls. It is the time when the earth has its mantle of snow and surrenders to its crystallizing forces, when mankind can be united with the earth as the thinking earth-body in the cosmos. Then the souls pass out of the cosmos and assemble, as it were, in the earth-sphere. This is the annual impregnation of the earth's seasonal being.

If we have insight not only into the physical aspect of the cosmos but into the activities of those cosmic beings I have described for you in the four pictures, then we arrive at all these things. And with this insight we can find some indications of cosmic creativity in many a poem, for it is there in the world:

How each the Whole its substance gives,
each in the other works and lives!
See heavenly forces rising and descending,
their golden urns reciprocally lending:
on wings that winnow sweet blessing
from heaven through the earth they're pressing,
to fill the All with harmonies caressing.

In these very words we can feel something of that wonderful working in one another and with one another of the four Archangel beings who, in conjunction with the forces of nature, also live and weave in the body, soul and spirit of mankind.

Publisher's Note Regarding Rudolf Steiner's Lectures

The lectures contained in this volume have been translated from the German which is based on stenographic and other recorded texts that were in most cases never seen or revised by the lecturer. Hence, due to human errors in hearing and transcription, they may contain mistakes and faulty passages. Every effort has been made to ensure that this is not the case. Some of the lectures were given to audiences more familiar with anthroposophy; these are the so-called 'private' or 'members' lectures. Other lectures, like the written works, were intended for the general public. The difference between these, as Rudolf Steiner indicates in his *Autobiography*, is twofold. On the one hand, the members' lectures take for granted a background in and commitment to anthroposophy; in the public lectures this was not the case. At the same time, the members' lectures address the concerns and dilemmas of the members, while the public work speaks directly out of Steiner's own understanding of universal needs. Nevertheless, as Rudolf Steiner stresses: 'Nothing was ever said that was not solely the result of my direct experience of the growing content of anthroposophy. There was never any question of concessions to the prejudices and preferences of the members. Whoever reads these privately printed lectures can take them to represent anthroposophy in the fullest sense. Thus it was possible without hesitation—when the complaints in this direction became too persistent—to depart from the custom of circulating this material "for members only". But it must be borne in mind that faulty passages do occur in these reports not revised by myself.' Earlier in the same chapter, he states: 'Had I been able to correct them [the private lectures] the restriction [for members only] would have been unnecessary from the beginning.'

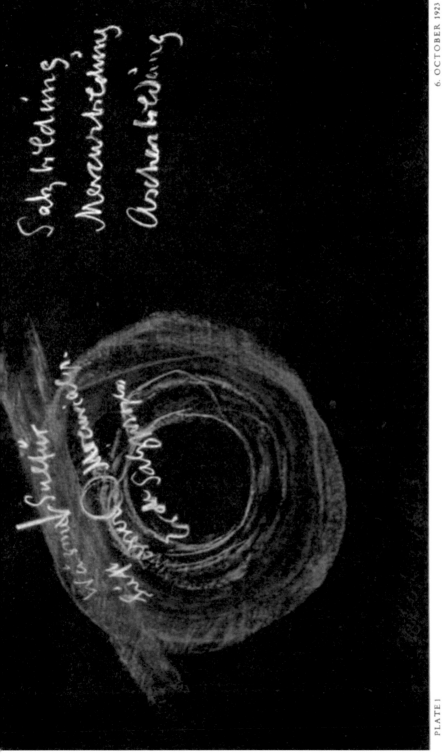

PLATE 1

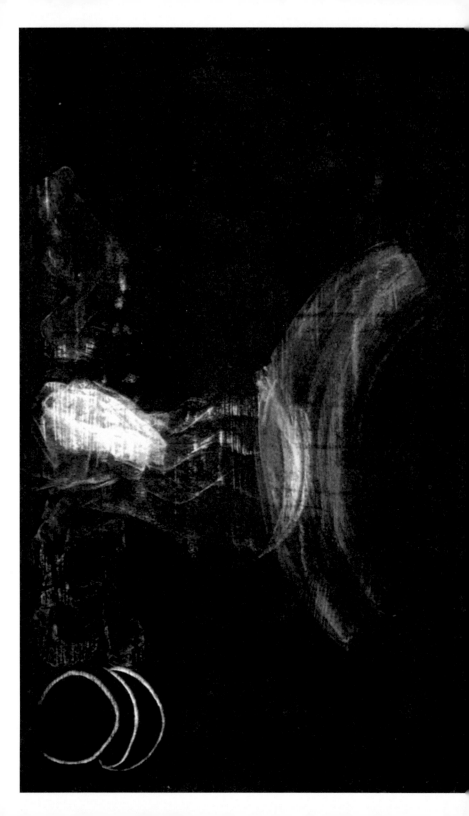

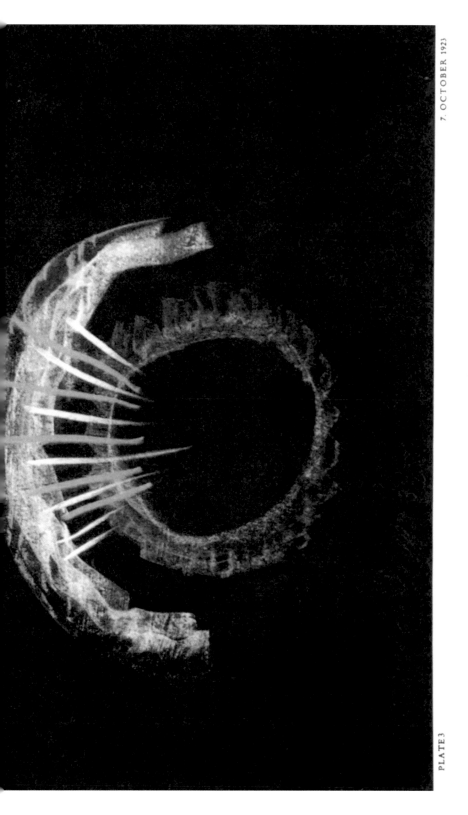

PLATE 3

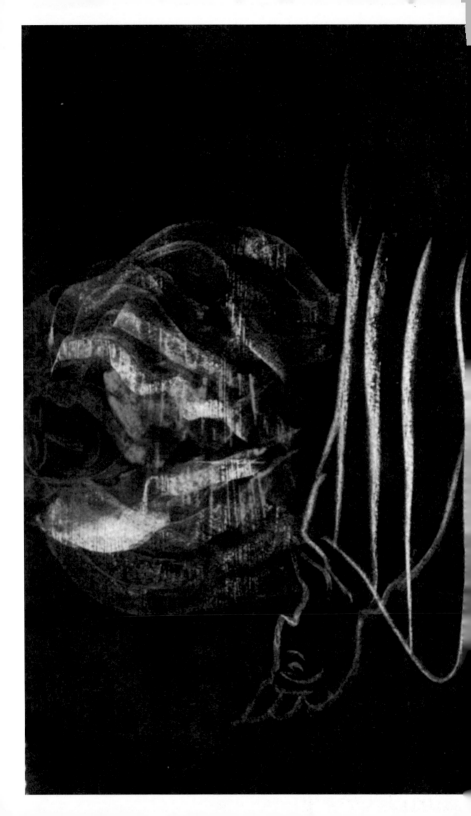